LIKE A MOTH TO A FLAME

LIKE A MOTH TO A FLAME

**Good Girls Who Are
Attracted to Bad Boys**

Dr William J. Allender

NEW
HOLLAND

First published in 2022 by New Holland Publishers
Sydney

Level 1, 178 Fox Valley Road, Wahroonga, NSW 2076, Australia

newhollandpublishers.com

A record of this book is held at the National Library of Australia.

ISBN 9781760794415

Group Managing Director: Fiona Schultz
Publisher: Lesley Pagett
Project Editor: Liz Hardy
Designer: Andrew Davies
Production Director: Arlene Gippert
Printed in Australia by IVE Group

10 9 8 7 6 5 4 3 2 1

Keep up with New Holland Publishers:

 NewHollandPublishers
 @newhollandpublishers

'Thus Hath the Candle Singed the Moath,'
William Shakespeare, *The Merchant of Venice*

Dedicated to the female victims of the crimes and their long-suffering families.

Contents

'Controllers, abusers and manipulative people
don't question themselves.
They don't ask themselves if the problem is them.
They always say the problem is someone else.'

Darlene Ouimet, *Emerging from Broken*

Introduction

Many times while waiting to give evidence outside a courthouse, I've wondered why so many intelligent young women, the 'good girls' from stable homes, get themselves mixed up with men of ill repute, the 'bad boys' of society. Could it be that despite the fact the young women's parents would have told them to stay away from exactly those types of people, there is something mysterious and dark about the men that young women can't quite put their finger on and so they find themselves irresistibly drawn towards them?

There have been a number of theories as to why this is so. For example, 'bad boys' are forbidden. Eve wanted the forbidden fruit and 'good girls' want the forbidden fruit. And 'bad boys' are more exciting. They bring out the more adventurous side of a woman, allowing her to live a little more dangerously and do things that she never thought or believed she would do. As William Cowper wrote in *The Task*, his poem from 1795, 'Variety is the very spice of life that gives it all its flavour.'

But I think a heavily tattooed motorcycle gang member, a 'bikie', summed it up well to me, with a more modern day comment, 'They [the women] love the outlaw.' Well, a number of movies seem to support this notion as James Dean showed in *Rebel Without a Cause*, for example.

Another theory is that it's a girl's only way to rebel. She secretly wants to be bad, too, but doesn't have it in her to follow her desires. It's as close as she'll get to tarnishing her Little Miss Perfect image, while also driving her parents to despair at the same time!

Quite often though, women are driven by a nobler quest and think they can change their 'bad boys'. They hope to achieve their goal and turn them away from their antisocial ways. That's a more motherly approach. It's also a quest that quite often fails, as leopards rarely, if ever, change their spots. The latter stories in this series clearly illustrate this in the sad outcomes.

Those above-mentioned theories, among several others, are maybe why some 'good girls' are attracted to 'bad boys'. I think it's really one for the psychologists.

Unfortunately, matters become even more intense and extremely dangerous when drugs are involved in such relationships. Then, the 'moth' ventures too close to the 'flame' with the most disastrous results, often with serious injury (physical and/or mental) or, at its worst, even death. And that's when the forensic toxicologist and other specialists enter the scene.

In this book, I present a selection of case stories (some names have been changed for legal reasons) from the many I have been involved with over the years. Some have led to successful prosecutions and some haven't, and I hope that there may be readers who can help the police in their enquiries in the cases of the latter.

I have also included a number of earlier and later stories that I was not involved with because I see them as being relevant to the theme of the book in that they illustrate how dark forces, if not constrained, can dominate their victims to the point of ruin and very often death; hence the phrase and title of the book *Like a Moth to a Flame*, which means to be irresistibly and dangerously attracted to someone or something.

The stories that follow, particularly the latter ones, illustrate this phenomenon perfectly. But, more importantly, remind us that we need to protect the mothers, wives and children from the terrible aberrations which can occur when these relationships fail through the controlling actions of a misguided and/or murderous partners. The last story was particularly brutal, as not only an innocent wife was involved, but also their three beautiful children.

These stories span from 1908 to 2020 showing how little has changed in just over 11 decades, except for the punishment meted out to the villains when finally caught.

I hope you, the reader, find them both interesting and informative.

Dr William J. Allender
Forensic scientist
MSc; PhD; FRACI; FACBS

George Joseph Smith. *Source:* The National Archives, UK

1.
Brides in the Bath Murders

'A dog will look down when they have done wrong,
but a snake will look you right in the eyes.'

Anon

This case was significant in the realms of forensic pathology and science because similarities between connected crimes were used to prove intention, a technique used in many future prosecutions.

George Joseph Smith has been described as cunning, ruthless, conniving and unattractive. Not characteristics that would feature high on a woman's shopping list when looking for a husband, but in spite of that, Smith managed to seduce a number of young women and get them to marry him.

So what was his big attraction? Was it that he had that air of mystery and a 'bad boy' image?

Whatever it was, those women who did fall for his 'charms' all suffered in some way. Most lost their money and possessions, but they can count themselves lucky, as several paid with their lives. And eventually, because of that, so did Smith – by hanging.

George Joseph Smith was born on 11 January 1872 in Bethnal Green, in London's East End. He was a wrong 'un from the get-go, as they say. At the tender age of nine he was sent to a reformatory in Gravesend for stealing, where he stayed until the age of 16, no doubt learning a thing or two while resident there, as he later served time for swindling and theft. In 1896, he was again sent to prison, having influenced a woman to steal from her employers. He used the proceeds of the robbery to open a baker's shop in Leicester.

It was there that he met and married Caroline Beatrice Thornhill (who was to be his only legal wife), using the alias Oliver George Love, on 17 January 1898. They moved to London, where Caroline worked as a maid, with Smith making her steal money and goods from her various employers. Eventually, she was arrested after trying to sell some silverware that she'd stolen and she was subsequently sentenced to 12 months' imprisonment. Feeling that she'd received a raw deal, she sought some sort of redress, and so she turned, giving state evidence against Smith, who was implicated in the crime. He was arrested, and on 9 January 1901, he was sentenced to two years at Her Majesty's pleasure, in Hastings prison, for receiving stolen goods. In the meantime, Caroline Thornhill (Love) wisely migrated to Canada.

On his release, Smith looked for her unsuccessfully and so turned his attentions to his middle-aged boarding-house keeper. After 'marrying' her, he quickly relieved her of all her money and then looked around for another victim. She was Florence Wilson, a widow from Worthing. He 'married' her and took 30 pounds (in excess of 3000 English pounds by today's values) from her account as well as selling her belongings from her Camden residence in London. He used the proceeds from the sales to set himself up as a second-hand dealer, with a shop in Bristol.

On 30 July 1908, he 'married' again. This time it followed a quick romance, and the poor unfortunate woman was Edith Pegler, who had replied to his advertisement for a housekeeper.

As an antique dealer, Smith would often travel alone to various towns and cities, and on a visit to Southampton, he met a clerk by the name of Sarah Freeman, introducing himself as George Rose. Unfortunately, like her predecessors, she fell for Smith, and in October 1909, she became his next bigamous bride.

The couple moved to lodgings in London, where Smith persuaded Freeman to withdraw all her savings from a post office, a total of 260 pounds, and sell some of her government bonds to fund an antiques business. He rewarded her by taking her out for the day and then leaving her waiting at a venue while he returned to their lodgings to remove most of her belongings, which he subsequently sold, using the proceeds to purchase a second-hand-furniture shop in Southend.

Up to that point, larceny had been Smith's main pursuit, but that was about to change.

His next victim was the daughter of a banker. Her name was Beatrice (Bessie) Constance Annie Mundy. Her father had died in 1904 and left her what was a substantial estate for the time – 2500 pounds in gilt-edged securities. However, the estate was managed by her uncle, who allocated her the sum of just eight pounds per month on which to live. In spite of that, Smith, now calling himself Henry Williams, managed to swindle 135 pounds out of her estate before clearing off with the proceeds, leaving Beatrice to spend the next 18 months wondering what had happened to their relationship.

As luck would have it, in 1912, while she was staying in Weston-super-Mare, she chanced upon him once again, but instead of taking him to task over what he'd done, she welcomed him back. That was a huge mistake because Smith had worked out how to get access to her money.

In the meantime, they rented a small house in Herne Bay, Kent. On moving into the premises, Smith visited an ironmonger to purchase a cast-iron bath, as no suitable private bathing facilities were available in their new accommodation. At the same time, he also arranged for both of them to visit a solicitor and have their wills drawn up. In addition, he persuaded the solicitor to write to Bessie's uncle with words to the effect that they, Mr and Mrs Williams, had sorted out their differences and sought a stable life together, and that he supposedly strove to be a 'true and worthy husband'.

On Wednesday 10 July, on Smith's insistence, the trusting Bessie visited

Dr French, an inexperienced doctor. Smith told him that his wife had suffered from fits. At the same time, he had Bessie write to her uncle, saying her health wasn't good, but that her husband was 'showing her every possible kindness'.

Three days later, on 13 July, at about 7.30 am, Bessie decided to try out her new bath. Half an hour later, Dr French received an urgent message from Smith. 'Can you come at once? I'm afraid my wife may be dead.' On his arrival, Dr French saw Bessie in the bath, her head submerged in the water. The police were quickly notified and took statements from various witnesses.

Later that same day, Smith wired her family to tell them, 'Words cannot describe the great shock I suffered in the loss of my wife. The doctor said she had a fit in the bath.'

A subsequent inquest, held on 15 July, recorded a verdict of misadventure, and Bessie Williams was buried in a common grave the following day.

The 2500 pounds was eventually allocated to Smith after an unsuccessful bid to stop it by Bessie's relatives. He promptly used it to purchase several properties in Bristol and arranged an annuity for himself.

It was just over a year before he sought out his next victim. She was an attractive young lady who went by the name of Alice Burnham. They met in Southsea in late October. Alice was a 25-year-old private nurse, whose father was a fruit grower

Bessie Mundy died from 'misadventure' in 1912. *Source:* The National Archives, UK in Buckinghamshire. Surprisingly, Smith used his real name, but he was still very much the same person he'd always been.

They were married within a week, on 4 November 1913, at a Portsmouth registry office. Alice didn't have much money, but Smith managed to get about 130 pounds from her and her family. However, before their bigamous marriage, he insured her life for 500 pounds, and to further seal the deal, he persuaded her to make a will that left all her possessions to him.

On 10 December, they moved to Blackpool. On the very same day, Alice was suffering from headaches, so Smith took her to a Dr Billing for treatment. The following day, she felt tired, so in the evening, before they both went for a walk, Smith asked the landlady, Mrs Crossley, to prepare her a bath for when they returned.

A little later, at around 8.15 pm, water started seeping through the ceiling of the two-storey lodgings. It was coming from the bathroom upstairs. Mrs Crossley informed Smith, who was in the downstairs kitchen, and he took off up the stairs.

When he reached the bathroom he shouted out, 'Call the doctor! My wife cannot answer me!'

Dr Billings promptly arrived at the scene and examined the young woman in the bath, pronouncing her dead. A later inquest found that she'd died an 'accidental death'.

Smith subsequently received Alice's 500-pound life insurance payout, and after selling her goods, he moved back to his earlier 'wife' Edith Pegler, who was living in Bristol. It remains a mystery why she took him back after several prolonged absences, but she did, and together they travelled to various places in England before finally settling in Bournemouth.

While on a visit to London in early September 1914, Smith met up with another young lady. Her name was Alice Reavil and she was a servant girl. Smith introduced himself as Charles Oliver James, and after a whirlwind romance, he married her by special licence on 17 September. After honeymooning in Battersea, Smith persuaded her to withdraw 76 pounds from her savings account, and upon receiving the money, he simply left and returned to Edith Pegler.

Alice Burnham had apparently drowned in her bath in 1913. *Source:* London Metropolitan Archives

But still Smith wasn't finished.

On a visit to Bath, in June 1914, under the guise of an estate agent called John Lloyd, he met 38-year-old spinster Margaret Lofty, the daughter of a deceased clergyman. She was recovering from an earlier liaison with a man whom she'd discovered was already married. The irony! Smith sweet-talked her, and they got married on 17 December, taking up lodgings on the second floor of a two-storey house in Highgate, London.

Once settled in, Smith took his new wife to a doctor and then to a solicitor, where they drew up a will that left all her possessions to Smith. He also insured her life for 700 pounds.

That evening, just before 8 pm, Margaret decided to have a bath. A short time later the landlady, Lousia Blatch, heard the sound of splashing coming from directly above the kitchen. That was followed by a noise that sounded like someone grabbing the side of the bath, and then a sigh.

She thought it a little odd, but the noises quickly ceased and so she thought no more of them. However, she then heard the nineteenth century hymn 'Nearer, My God, to Thee' being played on the harmonium. Again, strange, but none of her business. That hymn is supposedly the one that was played as the *Titanic* sank, so was Smith demonstrating a streak of sick humour for yet another dying woman?

Shortly after, Smith left the house on the pretext of buying tomatoes for his and his wife's supper, and on his return, he had to knock on the front door in order to get back in again as he said he'd forgotten his key. He went upstairs and called out to his wife. Not receiving an answer, he knocked on the bathroom door. Then he called down to the landlady,

'My God! It's my wife! She doesn't answer. I do hope nothing has happened to her.'

Louisa Blatch went up to the bathroom and saw Smith trying to get his wife out of the bath. Clearly, she was dead, as her body was cold, her lips were blue and swollen, and froth was coming from her nose and mouth. A doctor was summoned, and as there were no signs of a struggle, the doctor who carried out the post-mortem surmised that Margaret had fainted in the bath and subsequently drowned.

Margaret Lofty's death was 'accidental' in 1914. *Source:* The National Archives, UK

She was buried on 21 December, with an inquest again finding for an accidental death. Once more, Smith went back to Edith Pegler.

But his luck was about to take a turn for the worse.

Details of Margaret's death appeared in the national press, where they caught the eye of Alice Burnham's father, Charles. He immediately thought that there was a strong similarity between his daughter's death and that of Margaret, and with that in mind, he forwarded the news article to Mr Redhead of the Aylesbury police. In addition, in January 1915, he sent several newspaper clippings about both the Blackpool and Highgate cases to Detective Inspector Aurthur Neil of Scotland Yard, asking him to investigate, which he did, discovering that George Smith, Henry Williams and John Lloyd were all the same person.

On 4 January, Smith, keen to collect his wife's life insurance, went to his solicitor and left instructions that his departed wife's life insurance policy should be finalised. But in the meantime, Scotland Yard detectives were alerted.

When Smith returned to the solicitor's office on 1 February to collect his ill-gotten earnings, Detective Inspector Arthur Neill and two police sergeants from Scotland Yard were waiting for him. He was duly questioned about his identity and movements.

'Are you John Lloyd?' Inspector Neill asked.

'Er, yes,' Smith replied.

The inspector then outlined the various events leading up to him marrying Margret Lofty in December and finding her drowned in a bath at his lodgings in Highgate.

'Yes, quite right.' Smith said.

But there were more questions to come.

'Are you also said to be identical with George Smith, whose wife was also found dead under similar circumstances on 11th December, 1913, in Blackpool?'

'Smith?' Smith replied. 'I'm not Smith. I don't know what you are talking about.'

He was then taken into custody.

He was interviewed at the police station with regard to his activities, and he eventually admitted he was the George Smith who had married Alice Burnham. With that revelation, he was then charged with, '… causing a fake entry relating to a marriage between himself as John Lloyd and Margaret Elizabeth Lofty, at the registry office, Bath, on 17 December, last.'

However, the police still had no solid evidence of murder, but given the suspicious circumstances, an order was given that the unfortunate women's bodies had to be exhumed – a most unpleasant task and quite harrowing for their relatives.

Dr Bernard Henry Spilsbury, a Home Office pathologist, was called in to examine the bodies of the women. In what was a truly puzzling case, no drugs were detected in their bodies and the young ladies all appeared to be fit, not having any of the health issues alleged by Smith, apart from headaches and fits. Furthermore, there was no evidence of foul play, such as a struggle before death. But as a pathologist, Spilsbury knew that a sudden rush of water into the nose and throat can stimulate the vagus nerve, which connects the brain to the heart, and that sudden stimulation causes the nerve to send a signal to the heart to stop, ensuring death. The answer appeared to lie in the baths in which the victims had died. But how could they have resulted in their deaths?

Dr Spilsbury believed that it would be almost impossible for an adult suffering from a fit or faint to drown in the narrowing, tapering baths that were available at the time, and he presented various documents to illustrate his point:

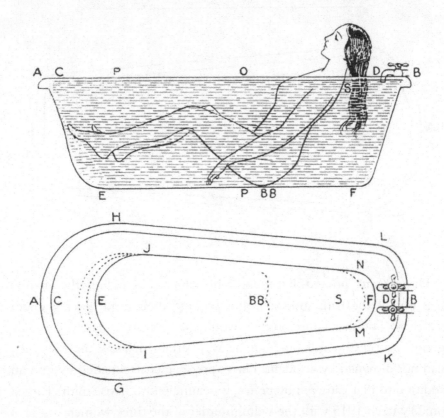

But more importantly, he was surprised by the observation that Bessie Mundy had been holding on to a bar of soap when she'd been found dead. If she had really suffered a fit or faint, as the inquest had suggested, her hand would have released the soap into the bath water. That evidence suggested that she, and probably the other victims, had died very suddenly, without time to put up any resistance.

It appeared to be a very clever strategy with which Smith had dispatched his various 'wives'. But that posed a further quesion: How did he do it?

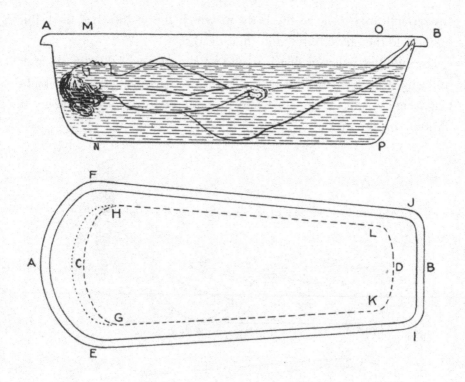

Dr Spilsbury posited that it could be achieved by pulling the victim's legs out of the bath suddenly, thus sending their head quickly under water, so fast that consciousness would be lost immediately, certainly giving no time to call out. But he was certain that the three women had not drowned by accident. The expert evidence supplied by him, in addition to that gathered by police, was sufficient to have Smith charged on 23 March 1915 with the wilful murder of the three women.

The trial began on a bleak, cool and wet morning at the Old Bailey before Mr Justice Scrutton. Predictably, Smith pleaded not guilty.

It became quite a big event, being widely published in the media. A total of 264 exhibits were shown before the court and 112 witness were examined.

But the most extraordinary piece of evidence was the reconstruction of the alleged murders, organised by Inspector Neill in the anteroom of the court. To demonstrate Dr Spilsbury's theory of how Smith's victims were drowned, the inspector had a rather brave nurse, in a bathing costume, sit in a bath of a similar shape to those used by Smith's victims. A police officer then demonstrated the technique described by Dr Spilsbury. The nurse's body slid towards the end of the bath, with her head quickly being submerged in the bath water. Unfortunately, the woman immediately showed signs of drowning and had to be resuscitated.

The trial concluded on 1 July, and after considering an overwhelming amount of evidence against him, the jury took just 22 minutes to find Smith guilty. On learning the jury's verdict, Mr Justice Scrutton pronounced the only sentence possible – death by hanging.

George Smith's life ended in Maidstone Prison on Friday 13 August 1915, the conman, swindler, bigamist, and finally multiple murderer protesting his innocence to the bitter end. But the noose concluded his protests and his evil life.

Unfortunately, human nature being what it is, I have no doubt that attractive women will continue to meet up with such evil scoundrels in the future. One can only hope that they don't end up having to pay with their lives as the next story suggests.

Mamie Stuart, circa 1918. *Source: The Daily Mirror*, 1923

2.
The Chorus Girl Mystery:
Death of Mamie Stuart

'To betray you must first belong.'
Harold Philby

One wintery evening in 1920, a young couple were strolling along the cliffs above Brandy Cove, Caswell Bay, in south Wales, when they heard the agonised screams of a terrified woman. They appeared to be coming from beneath their feet, possibly from a cave, so braving the gathering dusk, they climbed down the cliff to render assistance to whoever was in distress. But despite spending some time looking for a cave and listening for further cries to locate the woman, no more were heard, leaving the perplexed and shaken couple free to continue their journey home.

The same happened a few weeks later, only that time, the cries were heard by a rock fisherman. A thorough search was carried out in the area to find the source of the distress, but to no avail.

Not long after, regular reports started to be made of a woman crying out in agony, particularly in the area of the very secluded Brandy Cove. It soon became apparent that this was no mortal woman in distress, but some poor agonised spirit. Stories of the screams soon became common talk amongst the surrounding villages of Bishopston, Pennard and Caswell, and as a consequence, the locals became too afraid to visit the beach after dark.

It wasn't until 5 November 1961 that the matter was resolved, and then only inadvertently, by three young men from Bishopston.

John Gerke, aged 25 and an experienced caver, had recently found a large air shaft in the cliffs off Brandy Cove and was eager to share the find with his two friends, Graham Jones, aged 26, and Colin McNamara, aged 24. Gerke was keen to introduce them, both non-cavers, to the pleasures and adventure of caving, which they planned on making a regular activity, so on that Sunday afternoon, the three of them checked out the air shaft, which was attached to a long abandoned lead mine.

It descended into the cliff to a depth of about 7 metres, at an angle of about 30 degrees, and at its base was a narrow enclosure in the rock strata. The three men climbed through with some difficulty, or as Gerke later told the local newspaper, 'We wriggled through and got into a sort of ante-chamber. It was about eight feet long, and leading off apparently to old workings was a tunnel, but the entrance was blocked by boulders. When we tried to shift them, we found that what looked like a solid wall was really only a slab about three inches thick, placed on end and resting on boulders and smaller stones behind.'

It was a very cramped situation, but Gerke was able to move the stones away from the entrance. With the rocky rubble cleared, he uncovered a horrifying secret – on top of a pile of animal bones was a human skull.

The discovery was immediately shared with the police, who accompanied the three men back to the cave, where they once more descended into the grim shaft. By means of a hand-to-hand chain, they passed their awful discoveries to the police for further examination. The grisly 'treasure trove' included skeletal remains as well as other artefacts found at the site – a rotted sack filled with more human bones, a hair clip which still had some brown hair attached to it, and a quantity of jewellery still in good condition. The exhibits were then taken to the Home Office Forensic Science Laboratory in Cardiff for further examination.

From the outset, a local newspaper believed the skeletal remains to be those of Mamie Stuart, a 26-year-old brunette, who had disappeared from her home in Caswell 40 years previously, but it was up to the forensic investigators to positively establish the identity of the deceased.

The bones were examined by Dr Lester James, a Home Office pathologist, and Brian Morgan, a forensic scientist. From the configuration of the skull and the pelvis, the remains were identified as belonging to a young female, but worse still, it appeared that the skeleton had been sawn inexpertly into three roughly equal lengths before being walled into the cave.

There were a lot of saw cuts across the skeletal bones, with cuts across both upper arms and along the spine and shoulder blades, and the legs had been severed by more saw cuts. The attempt to dispose of the body appeared to have been frenzied. (I was involved in a disturbingly similar case many years later, which I outlined in my book *The Expert Witness*.)

The skeleton was reassembled and the individual limb bones measured before its height was estimated at about 5 feet 4 inches. The woman's age was calculated by determining the growth areas in the bones, which appeared to have reached maturity, indicating it to be somewhere in the mid-twenties. X-ray examination of the skull showed that two bones at the base had only recently joined, and together with three wisdom teeth, it indicated that the woman was probably no more than 28 at the time of her death. Unfortunately, because so many years had passed since her death, there were no body organs or soft tissue, so it wasn't possible to determine how she'd died.

The bits of jewellery and clothing found in the sack, together with the bones, proved useful in identifying their former owner. There was a wedding and engagement ring, both bearing hallmarks that placed them at between 1912 and 1918, and some gilt-copper tassels, which had been fashionable in the 1920s, when they'd been worn on the end of a fur stole. In addition, an old friend of Mamie (Amy) Stuart, with a long memory, identified the articles as belonging to her friend.

Finally, a life-sized picture of Mamie was superimposed on the skull, and it was an almost perfect match. With a positive identification of the deceased made, the investigation moved on to determine how her remains had wound up in her awful tomb and who the culprit was who had carried out the evil deed and dumped her broken body where they obviously hoped it would never be found.

A search of the newspaper records about the time Mamie Stuart went missing provided valuable background information. It became apparent that even in 1920, police had been convinced that Mamie Stuart, confirmed age of 26, had been murdered, but they'd had no suspect and no corpse. The story of Mamie Stuart was soon to be unravelled.

In 1908, at the age of 15, and much to her parents' disapproval, she left her home in Sunderland to pursue a career on the stage. She was an accomplished singer, dancer and pianist. She spent a number of years singing and dancing in concert on various billings in theatres around Britain, during which time she kept contact with her family and visited them regularly.

Mamie Stuart's dance group where she was a chorus girl. Mamie was fourth from the right. *Source:* UK Archives

Things started looking up for her after she formed a troupe known as the Verona Girls, as they began to receive regular theatrical engagements. Unfortunately, several mishaps affected the troupe, including one of the girls breaking an ankle, and it was during that low point in her career that Mamie met George Shotton, also from Sunderland. Although he was 13 years her senior, she fell heavily for him, and after a brief romance, the couple married in a Swansea registry office on 25 March 1918. They honeymooned in Droitwich Spa before settling into their new home in Bayswater, Swansea.

But unknown to Mamie, Shotton had a dark secret: he was already married and not the widower he claimed to be. His wife's name was Mary (nee Leader), also known as May, whom he'd married on 7 September 1905, in Newport, south Wales. He lived with her and his son Arthur in Penarth (near Cardiff) prior to meeting Mamie.

George Shotton was a marine surveyor, and because of the nature of his work, he spent a good deal of his time away from his family, travelling around the country on business, which turned out to be a very convenient way to lead two different lives.

Before setting up home in Bayswater, he and Mamie moved several times; first to Bristol and then on to Swansea. No doubt, the locations were chosen by Shotton to maintain and conceal his deception from both his lawful wife and Mamie.

Their home in Swansea was managed by a Mrs Hearn, who became a confidante to Mamie during George's regular lengthy absences. Mamie often spoke of her regrets at getting married and her desire to go back to London and return to the stage that she

George Shotton and Mamie Stuart in happier times. *Source:* The National Archives, UK

loved. She greatly missed the spotlights and the glamour associated with her career, and that conflict caused numerous arguments during George's stays at the boarding house. In addition, Mamie had a flirtatious personality and was a bit of a social butterfly, which added further pressure to the 'marriage'.

It was sometime later that a letter from George Shotton was sent to his 'wife' Mamie, written around 25 July 1919:

You ask to be free. Are you not more free than any other girl?

You wander to and fro at your own sweet will, no-one to question or prohibit you. Now you see that such is not what you ought to do.

I do not quite understand in what manner I could do more. It does not lie in my power. I have no intention of doing such awful things as you suggest.

I can only imagine you mean me to go on the wrong path so that you can divorce me. I will not believe that you have ever done anything that I could complain about.

I gave myself to you long ago. You never seemed to care after a few short weeks. I did my best for you. I gave you my name and my love, and you trifled with both.

To ease the stress, a change of scenery appeared to be the temporary solution, so the bigamous couple moved into a villa called Ty-Llanwydd (ironically translated as the 'Abode of Peace'), close to Brandy Cove, on the Gower Peninsula, in November 1919. On 12 November that year, Mamie sent a postcard to her parents, who duly replied, only to have their letter returned, marked 'House Closed'.

Certain that there must have been some mistake, Mamie's father sent a reply-paid telegram to the Ty-Llanwydd address, but that, too, was returned by the post office.

Clearly, something was amiss. But there, unfortunately, the matter rested.

The following year, 1920, an unknown man left a large leather trunk at the Grosvenor Hotel, College Street, in Swansea. It was still there on 20 March, so the hotelier notified the police. Inside the trunk were various items of jewellery, a pair of shoes, a Bible, a rosary and a manicure set. But of more interest were a pair of boots and two dresses, both inexplicably torn and cut into pieces. At the bottom of the trunk was a piece of paper bearing the Sunderland address of Mamie's parents, who subsequently identified the contents as belonging to their daughter.

It was all very suspicious, and the resulting investigation fingered George Shotton as the main, if not the only, suspect implicated in Mamie's disappearance. A search of the Ty-Llanwydd premises, where George and Mamie had stayed, revealed a mildewed brown leather handbag containing a few pounds in loose change, and, more importantly, a ration card issued to Mamie Stuart.

At that point, Inspector William Draper from Scotland Yard arrived to look into a case that was increasingly shaping up to be a murder investigation. His first step was to determine the whereabouts of George Shotton, the bigamous husband. Fortunately, the police didn't have to look too far, as he was living in an isolated house in Caswell Bay, just under 2 miles from Ty-Llanwydd, with his legal wife and their toddler son.

When he was interviewed by police, his story was simple. 'Yes sir, I did live with Mamie Stuart. No I didn't marry her, and no, I don't know where she is now.'

He admitted that they'd had arguments, but said they'd just parted company and gone their separate ways – he back to his wife, and Mamie, to who knows where.

Although George Shotton appeared to be a mild-mannered gentleman, he was said to have a bad temper and was very jealous of Mamie's flirtatious ways, which was a bit rich, considering he was married legally to another woman, and according to reports, his jealousy fuelled a stormy relationship, particularly in the days prior to Mamie's sudden disappearance.

As it was, Shotton was put on trial on 3 June 1920, to answer charges about his bigamous marriage. The evidence against him was overwhelming, and on 27 July, he was convicted and sentenced to 18 months of hard labour in Swansea prison. In the meantime, the police harboured suspicions that he'd murdered Mamie Stuart, and began to dig up the gardens in, and remove fireplaces from, his home in a search for her body. As a consequence, Shotton's wife and son moved into the George Hotel, Mumbles, a short distance from Swansea, where she initiated divorce proceedings. Despite their best efforts, the police found nothing, and no forensic evidence with which to implicate and prosecute Shotton.

The press ran a number of speculative stories, some linking Mamie Stuart to various men in the area and one even claiming that she'd travelled to India. Unsurprisingly, none were substantiated, and eventually, Mamie Stuart's disappearance faded from the news.

That was, until her remains were found in November 1961.

An inquest was held at Gowerton on 14 December to determine her cause of death, when it happened and who was responsible. Finally, some sort of justice was about to emerge.

The forensic evidence that was produced was able to determine the approximate time of her death and, more importantly, her killer, but because there was no soft tissue left on the skeleton, the cause of death was never established. As no bullets were found within the skeleton, it seemed that strangulation and/or stabbing was the most probable cause, although a cerebral haemorrhage resulting from homicidal violence couldn't be discounted.

However, evidence concerning her murderer clearly pointed to her bigamous husband, George Shotton. That was supported by some surprising evidence provided by a retired 83-year-old Swansea postman, who had delivered mail to the couple at Brandy Cove. He recalled that on one occasion, he'd seen Shotton outside Ty-Llanwydd, struggling with a bulky sack that he was attempting to put into the back of a van. When he'd asked if he could be of assistance, Shotton had replied, 'No, no, no! Oh God, you gave me a fright, I thought you were a policeman!'

The rotted sacking and its contents, found by the cavers, suggested that the postman had encountered Shotton as he'd been about to dispose of its grisly contents in the nearby lead mine. Unfortunately, the postman hadn't reported the incident at the time to the police, even though he'd thought it suspicious.

Further evidence was presented regarding Shotton's movements after his release from prison back in the 1920s. He appeared to have lived in London until 1938, when he again wound up in prison, that time for holding up his sister with a gun. He was later found working for a Bristol aircraft company and appeared to be living a low-profile, normal life as a 'respected' citizen.

Unfortunately, it wasn't possible to bring him to trial for the murder of Mamie Stuart, as when police finally tracked him down, he was already

6-feet underground in Bristol's Arnos Vale Cemetery. He'd died of natural causes in 1958, aged 78, thereby avoiding 'having his collar felt' (hanging) by three years.

Even though justice was never seen to have been done for Mamie's murder, no more ghostly cries were ever heard at Brandy Cove after her inquest. Sadly, her remains were never buried, but kept in a box at Cardiff University, where the eminent pathologist Bernard Knight would sometimes display them to his students. Unfortunately, her remains were last seen in 2007, and have since disappeared from storage to who knows where.

Rest in peace, dancing moth.

Florence Linda Agostini. *Source:* National Library of Australia

3.
The 'Pyjama Girl' Mystery:
The Murder of Linda Agostini

'Murder is an inherently evil act,
no matter what the circumstances.
No matter how convincing the rationalizations.'
Bentley Little, *The Ignored*

After a brief heavy rainfall the previous evening, it was a pleasant spring morning on 1 September 1934 when a young farmer, Tom Griffiths, was proudly walking home his family's new prize bull just outside the country town of Albury, New South Wales, and came across a gruesome discovery.

It was the body of a young woman that had been unceremoniously partially shoved into a culvert under the road in Splitter's Creek, along Howlong Road, near Albury, and had previously been doused with kerosene and then set alight. Heavy rainfall the night before had prevented completion of the ghastly process.

A strong smell of kerosene still lingered in the air, and it was evident to the young farmer that this flammable liquid had been used in an attempt to finally destroy the corpse. Albury police were quickly alerted, and so began one of Australia's longest and most shocking murder investigations.

Albury police investigators examining the site where the charred body was found. The deceased was subsequently known as the 'Pyjama Girl'. *Source:* NLC Archives

An Albury medical examiner found that the badly burnt body had been placed in a hessian bag and the victim's head was wrapped in a towel. Her body, when found, was clad in yellow-coloured, luxurious silk fabric clothing. She had been shot with a small calibre bullet which had lodged in her throat, and had been savagely beaten around the head. The bullet was extracted from her body and identified as coming from a .25 Webley & Scott automatic pistol.

However, the medical examiner concluded that the severe injuries to her skull and brain were the main cause of her death. She was described as being between the ages of 20 and 30, with light brown hair, blue-grey eyes and of slim build.

But it was the clothing she wore in her final hours that was so unusual.

The fabric remnants were identified as the remains of yellow and green silk pyjamas with a Chinese dragon motif. The oriental-style pyjamas that the dead woman wore resulted in her soon being dubbed the 'Pyjama Girl' by the media.

Her body was initially stored at the Albury morgue, where many people viewed her but none recognised her, most probably because her face had been so terribly damaged.

In the meantime, a sketch, altered to make her more lifelike, and a modified photograph of her corpse were circulated in the newspapers. But with no success. Amazingly, her identity was to remain unknown for about a decade.

It was then an extraordinary decision was made to preserve her body in formalin (formaldehyde) and place it in a zinc-lined bath. The body was moved to the Faculty of Medicine at Sydney University. It was here that over the years until 1942 her body was viewed by many hundreds of people, who were still unable to identify her. Sadly, it proved to be a fruitless, macabre display of a murder victim to the public. Her body was later transferred to police headquarters where it stayed until 1944.

However, a number of witnesses came forward and stated that the partly charred corpse appeared to resemble two missing women, Anna Philomena and Linda Agostini, the latter in particular. Subsequently, Antonio ('Tony') Agostini, her husband, was questioned by detectives assigned to the case, but Tony said that his wife had left him and he had no idea where she had gone. However, when pressed later, he said she had taken on a job as a hairdresser on a ship. He later moved to Perth and in January 1938 to Sydney, where he gained work as a waiter at a fashionable Italian restaurant known as Romano's.

In 1938 a coroner's inquest failed to establish the identity of the body. The dental records, a vital piece of evidence, didn't appear to match those of Linda Agostini.

In June 1940, Antonio Agostini was interned as an alien during World War II and spent time at various internment camps at Orange, Hay and Loveday (this latter camp was the largest internment camp and was built to house German, Italian and Japanese interns and prisoners of war) until 1944. He was released in February 1944 and returned to Romano's and took up his former position as a waiter. In reality, Agostini was a university-educated man and spent most of his working career in Australia as a journalist, in both Sydney and Melbourne, for the Italian newspaper, *Il Giornale Italiano*, and because of its Italian Fascist Party leanings, he found himself in the internment camps, as he appeared at the time to pose a threat to Australia. It was while working at Romano's that he met up with Police Commissioner, William John MacKay, a regular patron of the restaurant.

This was in early March 1944, when the police had a breakthrough for the case from several unexpected sources. Firstly, errors were discovered in examination of original dental records, which had noted six fillings, similar to Anna Philomena, but there were later found to be eight, matching those of Linda Agostini, whom police still had on file as a missing person. When the body was removed from the formalin bath, two porcelain fillings fell out of her teeth. The dental work had been done so well that it had been missed by previous examinations!

Further, several people who knew Linda recognised freckles on her upper arm which matched earlier photographs taken of her. In addition, William John MacKay, commissioner of the New South Wales police, had visited Romano's restaurant on many occasions. On this particular day, he recognised Antonio (Tony) Agostini, whom he knew before the war, and was surprised to see how unnerved and worried he seemed on seeing him. MacKay asked him what was wrong and it was then the whole sorry story came spilling out.

Tony Agostini broke down and admitted to having accidentally killing his wife.

On 4 March 1944 Agostini was formally interviewed by Police Commissioner William MacKay and Antonio (Tony) confessed to his involvement in his wife's death 10 years earlier. He provided a lengthy and detailed statement where he said that Linda died from a bullet wound, but said nothing of her severe head wounds, apart from saying that he may have dropped her body while conveying it to the motor vehicle for disposal. But there were to be discovered many inconsistences in his lengthy and detailed statement – and the whole case in general.

Tony Agostini was an Italian immigrant who came to Australia in 1927. He was born on 20 May 1903 at Altivole, Treviso, Italy. In 1928 he met Linda Platt, who was working part-time as a cinema usherette and her regular job was that of a hairdresser. She was born on 12 September 1905 at Forest Hill, London. Linda had migrated to New Zealand in 1926 and then onto Australia the following year. Linda was quite taken by the trim, dark-haired Italian and Tony by the attractive, petite brunette. They married in Sydney at the Registrar General's office on 22 April 1930. But the marriage was not a happy one.

It appeared that Linda in her early 'flapper' days, before she had met Tony, had grown fond of alcoholic beverages, and had developed a drinking problem. It was his wife's drinking problem that Tony Agostini said was the reason they moved to Melbourne in 1933, mainly to get her away from her drinking friends and their influence. But the change of location apparently had little effect, as her drinking continued and it made his life a misery. It was on a Monday morning that the situation further deteriorated, when he was abruptly woken by Linda pressing the barrel of a pistol to his head. In the ensuring struggle that occurred the gun had gone off, killing Linda.

Antonio Agostini said he could not bring himself to report the death to the police nor bear the shame that the death would have brought upon himself and the Italian community. He then decided to take the matter into his own hands.

Linda's body was loaded into the car and he drove over the state border to Albury, where he dumped her body in a culvert at Howlong, west of Albury, pouring petrol over her body and setting fire to it to dispose of the evidence. Then, after the ghastly deed, Agostini hurriedly returned to Melbourne.

Tony Agostini was arrested on 6 March 1944 and committed in April of that year to stand trial for murder at Sydney Supreme Court. At last it seemed the 'Pyjama Girl' case was coming to a conclusion.

In June that year, evidence presented to the court included, Antonio Agostini admitting that he had accidentally shot his wife with a gun but said nothing about inflicting severe head injuries on her, apart from possibly dropping her body down stairs. He told of the subsequent events that followed where he pushed her body into a culvert outside Albury and set fire to it. There was much discussion as to whether the bullet or head injuries had been the cause of her death. Leading experts were certain that the head injuries could not have been caused accidentally but were most likely due to the infliction of a number of heavy blows.

Despite this latter evidence, the jury returned a verdict of manslaughter after less than two hours of deliberation. Justice (Sir) Charles Lowe sentenced Antonio Agostini to six years' imprisonment with hard labour.

On 21 August 1948, Agostini was released from Pentridge Prison under a general amnesty after serving just under four years and was deported to Italy. He later married a widow, Giuseppina Gasoni in December 1952 at Cagliari, Sardinia. He died there in 1969 and was buried in San Michele Cemetery. While earlier, Linda Agostini had been buried in Preston Cemetery on 13 July 1944 at state expense.

There the matter appeared to end; but for a number of nagging inconsistent pieces of evidence that surfaced later. The 'Pyjama Girl' had grey-blue eyes and was small-breasted, while Ms Agostini's eyes were brown and her breasts were larger. At an earlier inquest, expert witnesses proposed that Linda's brown eyes could have turned blue after death, and that her breasts could have shrunk after being burnt. Apart from blue eyes turning brown (the opposite of what was observed), the evidence was unconvincing. Further, Antonio had stated that he used petrol to incinerate the body where in fact kerosene had been used on the body dubbed the 'Pyjama Girl'.

Doubts have been raised as to whether the body truly belonged to Linda Agostini, or whether she was coincidentally murdered around the same time as the 'Pyjama Girl' and the police used Antonio Agostini to close a high-profile case.

In 2004, the possibility of DNA testing of the corpse was raised in the hope that the mystery might be solved once and for all. However, NSW police would not agree to reopen the case because Antonio Agostini had confessed to the crime, the matter had gone before the court and 'all exhibits had been archived appropriately'.

Unfortunately, I have to agree, for quite a different reason: the body of the 'Pyjama Girl' was stored in formalin and on display for several years, then buried for 60 years. Formalin (or formaldehyde) denatures protein, rendering DNA sequencing impossible, thus, destroying any likelihood of testing her tissues – even her teeth. Sadly, end of story.

Elizabeth ('Beth') Short. *Source:* Hulton Archive (Getty Images)

4.

The Black Dahlia:
Who Murdered Elizabeth Short?

'The darkness of the soul is not lighted
by moving the body to another place.'

Eastern Proverb

There is an infamous and apparently still unsolved 1947 American murder case involving Elizabeth 'Beth' Short, a beautiful young woman who died at the tender age of 22. Her murder was so shocking that it even affected the crime-hardened Los Angeles society very deeply, and the horrid circumstances of her death still linger to this day.

She became known as 'The Black Dahlia'; a title that alluded not just to the mystery of her death, but also to her choice of dark clothes and her beautiful head of distinctive raven-black hair. Like a moth to a flame, Elizabeth was attracted to the bright lights of Hollywood, where she met someone who was most likely a 'very bad boy', and who subsequently took her life. But the circumstances of her death were very bizarre, to say the least.

Elizabeth was born on 29 July 1924 in Boston, Massachusetts. She was the third of five daughters of Cleo and Phoebe Short. Cleo Short was a man before his time, succeeding in making a prosperous living by designing and building miniature golf courses. Unfortunately, the Depression caught up with him, along with many others, and in 1929 he fell upon hard times and lost most of his savings, leaving the family in dire straits. In 1930, his car was found abandoned on Charlestown Bridge. It was assumed at the time he had committed suicide by leaping into the Charles River, but in actual fact, he had left his wife and five daughters and faked his suicide. Phoebe was left to deal with the loss and raise the girls by herself.

It was a tough call, but to her credit, she worked several jobs, including one as a bookkeeper and another and as a clerk in a bakery shop. Then, in 1942, she received a letter from Cleo, who was now living in California. He apologised for leaving her and the five children and asked to come back. Not unsurprisingly, after 12 difficult years, Phoebe refused to have anything to do with him.

However, Beth (also known as Betty to her family and friends) was of a more forgiving nature and decided to maintain contact with him. She was growing up to be very attractive young woman, and looked older and more sophisticated than she really was. However, she had health issues, being troubled by bronchitis, along with severe asthma attacks, and underwent lung surgery at the age of 15. Consequently, she was advised to move to a milder climate to ease her respiratory problems and so, when she turned 18, she accepted an offer from her father to move to Vallejo, California.

At the time, Cleo was working at the Mare Island naval shipyard in San Francisco Bay. Beth moved in with him, but the arrangement between them didn't work out, resulting in her moving out in January 1943. After that setback, she landed a job as a cashier at the Base Exchange in Camp Cooke (now known as Vandenberg Air Force Base), Lompoc, California, while living with several girlfriends. It wasn't long before her good looks were noticed by the servicemen, and she won the title of 'Cutie of Camp Cooke' in a beauty contest.

Beth wasn't a promiscuous young woman and wanted a permanent relationship, preferably with an airman. After several uneasy encounters, she left Lompoc and moved in with a girlfriend who lived in Santa Barbara. It was there that she had her only encounter with the law. On 23 September 1943, while with a group of noisy friends, she was arrested for underage drinking at a local restaurant. She was 19 and the minimum age for the legal consumption of alcoholic drinks was 21. She was booked and fingerprinted, but not charged.

It was arranged for her to go back to Massachusetts, but she went to Florida instead, where she met her beloved pilot, Major Matthew M. Gordon Jr, a decorated US Army Air Force officer. He was undergoing training for deployment to the China Burma India theatre of operations during World War II. They became engaged, and for a time things were looking up for Beth. Then tragedy struck. Major Gordon was posted overseas to India and died in an air crash on 10 August 1945, just a week short of the Japanese surrender which ended the war.

Beth was devastated, and after a period of mourning, she returned to Los Angeles in July 1946, later moving in with a friend, Dorothy French, who lived in the neighbourhood of Pacific Beach. One day, while in the Hollywood Canteen, a club for servicemen, she met up with Army Air Force Lieutenant Joseph G. Fickling, whom she knew from her time in Florida. She saw him as a possible replacement for her deceased fiancé, but when he kept pressuring her for sex, she finished the relationship. She was determined to save herself for marriage, whereas Fickling had no intention of making such a commitment.

But Beth was a dreamer, and she loved to go to nightclubs in Los Angeles that were frequented by film stars. In order to stand out and possibly attract the attention of agents and film producers, she dyed her brown hair raven black and started to wear tight dresses and black shoes to contrast with her milk-white complexion. To top off the effect, she wore a dahlia behind her ear, and it wasn't long before she was given the moniker, 'The Black Dahlia'.

She did manage to get some work as an extra in a few films, but that was all. Competition was fierce, as there were many good-looking girls like her, and she lacked the necessary talent and contacts. Suitable training would have solved the first of those requirements, but the second was more difficult. Contacts were necessary for any young hopeful if their dreams were to be realised, but some of the 'contacts' were not all they appeared to be, coming, as they did, from dubious backgrounds and masquerading as agents.

On the evening of 8 January 1947, Beth was picked up by a man called Robert 'Red' Morley from her friend's Pacific Beach apartment. He later dropped her off at the Biltmore Hotel in Los Angeles, where she was expecting to meet someone. He left her in the hotel lobby, where she made a telephone call, and that was the last time she was seen alive.

*

It was a sunny but cool morning on 15 January 1947 when Betty Bersinger took her three-year-old daughter for a walk in Leimert Park, Los Angeles. They were enjoying a pleasant stroll and laughing at the antics of the grey squirrels as they ran up and down the trees. Delightful creatures! But as they were passing a vacant allotment, Betty looked across and a white object caught her eye. She thought that maybe it was a discarded store mannequin, as the top and bottom were separated, but decided to go over and check it out, just in case.

She wasn't really expecting to see anything untoward, and so was horrified to find that it was actually a human corpse. She grabbed her daughter and hurried to a nearby house, where she telephoned the Los Angeles police department.

'I think I saw a dead body in a vacant lot at the west side of South Norton Avenue, midway between Coliseum Street and West 39th Street in Leimert Park,' she reported.

She went on to provide quite a bit of detail to the operator, which proved helpful to the police when they arrived at the scene a short time later. After pointing out the body and repeating the information she'd given over the phone, she left the scene feeling much shaken. Hers had been a gruesome discovery.

The body was clearly that of a female. It had been severely mutilated, severed at the waist and completely drained of blood, leaving the skin with a pallid white mannequin appearance, prior to being dumped in the vacant allotment. The body was in two pieces, separated by about 10 inches (approximately 25 centimetres) and had been placed in a posed position, with the hands placed over the head and the elbows bent at right angles, while the legs were spread apart.

And in a final act of cruelty, the once beautiful face had been slashed from the corners of the mouth to the ears, producing an effect known as the Glasgow smile, an evil act which is usually carried out with a utility knife or sometimes a piece of broken glass, leaving a horrible scar which causes the victim to appear to be, in a macabre way, smiling broadly.

As word seeped out, a crowd of people gathered, along with reporters and photographers from the *Los Angeles Herald-Express*, who took photographs of the corpse and crime scene. Everyone was asking the same questions: Who is she? Who could have done such an evil deed?

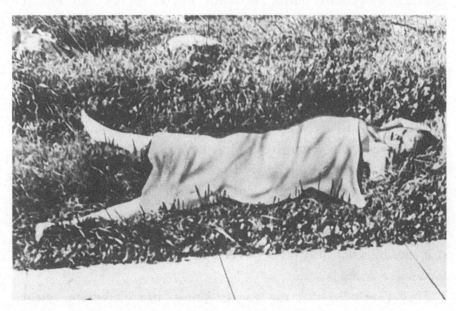

The naked corpse of the American aspiring actress and murder victim later identified as Elizabeth Short. The body was covered in a blanket shortly after police arrival. (The photograph was 'santised' to remove the very cruel facial disfigurement.)
Image: Archive Photos

Similar questions were later raised by the Los Angeles Police Department (LAPD).

A number of photographs were also taken by the Los Angeles crime scene team before the body was removed from the allotment and taken to the Los Angeles mortuary for post-mortem examination.

Artist Howard Burke sketched an idealised version of the murder victim, but the condition of the body was too awful for it to be printed in the *LA Examiner,* although a photo of the body *in situ* was subsequently published. The only way a picture of the crime scene could be printed was by manipulating the photo to remove the mutilations to the victim's face and adding a blanket to cover her. Essentially, the scene was artificially sanitised to avoid shocking readers with the true content of the disgusting crime.

The body arrived at the Los Angeles mortuary on 16 January 1947, and following an initial examination, it was found to have been hideously mutilated by cuts and burns. The burns inflicted on the body appeared to have been caused by a lit cigarette, and the cuts, while small, were deep and cruel. The body had also suffered several cuts to the breasts and thighs, where entire sections had been sliced away. Also, the initials BD had been carved deep in one thigh. Particular attention had been applied to the genital area and breasts, which had been partially shaved and slashed respectively. The Glasgow smile inflicted upon the victim measured about 7.5 centimetres on each side of her face. But worse still, it appeared that those injuries had occurred while the victim had still been alive. After death, the body had been bisected and the two halves of the corpse washed clean.

Judging by the knife cuts, the general opinion of the pathologists was that the dissection had possibly been carried out in a bath, with the victim in a sitting position.

They concluded that the young woman had died from cerebral haemorrhage, shock and/or blood loss, sometime between 9 pm on Tuesday 14 January and 3 am on the Wednesday when her body was subsequently found dumped in Leimert Park.

But who was she? Fingerprints provided the answer.

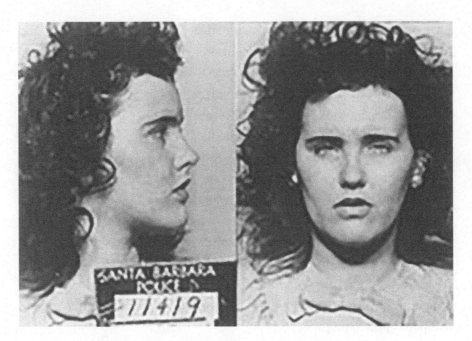

1943 mug shots of murder victim Elizabeth Short. Image: Archive Photos

Copies of the victim's fingerprints were sent to Washington DC via 'Soundphoto', an early form of fax machine for that era. The prints matched those given by Elizabeth Short when she'd been arrested in Santa Barbara for underage drinking

The horrible nature of the case made it top priority for the LAPD homicide squad under the leadership of Captain John Donahoe. Detectives soon traced Elizabeth's mother, who was still living in Medford, Massachusetts, and she subsquently had the awful task of identifying the body in the morgue. Such was the extent of facial mutilation, even Mrs Short found it difficult to recognise her own daughter.

But at least the victim's identity had been established. All police investigators had to do then was to find out who did the foul deed, and why.

Initially, there appeared to be only one real suspect, Robert 'Red' Manley, the man who dropped Beth off at the Biltmore Hotel a week before the discovery of her body. He was arrested and subjected to intense questioning, including lie-detector tests. Manley admitted he picked Elizabeth up from the Pacific Beach address on 8 January and that he spent the night with her in a motel after returning from a couple of nightspots. However, he slept on the bed, while Beth, who had said she was ill from possible food poisoning, slept in a lounge chair. The following day, he took her to the Biltmore Hotel in Los Angeles, where she supposedly expected to meet someone.

However, prior to his release from police custody, Manley said he'd seen scratches on her arms, but when he'd asked her about them, she'd replied that she had a friend who was intensely jealous. Manley was subsequently cleared.

The case eventually became a massive investigative task, with a total of 750 investigators from the LAPD and other departments working it alongside 400 sheriff's deputies and some 250 California State Patrol officers. Appeals to the public brought forth a lot of red herrings, which hampered police progress.

However, on 21 January 1947, just under a week after Elizabeth's body had been found, a man called the office of the *Los Angeles Examiner*, complaining to the editor about the coverage of the case and claiming to be the killer. He even offered to send him some of Elizabeth's belongings to prove he was who he said he was. And sure enough, a few days later, on 24 January, a manila envelope arrived at the newspaper's offices with a newsprint cut-and-paste message on the face of the envelope which read: 'Here is Dahlia's belongings Letter to follow'. Inside the envelope were Elizabeth Short's birth certificate, business cards, photographs and names written on various pieces of paper. But more importantly, there was an address book with the name Mark Hansen embossed on the cover. The package had been cleaned with petrol (gasoline), but several partial fingerprints were lifted from the envelope and sent to the Federal Bureau of Investigation for testing and matching. Unfortunately, the prints became compromised during transit and ceased to be of value.

However, it was clear from the disposal of Elizabeth's body in such a public place that the killer wanted his disgusting and cruel handiwork to be found. And that was a feature of the murder that was to persist throughout the police investigation, as he sent a further package of her clothes, and mocking letters were received by the media, all signed the 'Black Dahlia Avenger'.

On 27 January, the killer sent another letter to the *Los Angeles Examiner*, using cut-out newsprint to spell out the words 'Turning in Wed, Jan 29, 10am. Had my fun at police. Black Dahlia Avenger'. The police waited expectantly, thinking that 'turning in' meant 'turning myself in', but it wasn't to be. The grubby 'game' continued, and at 1 pm on the same day, a final note was received, which said, 'You would not give me a square deal. Dahlia killing was justified'. It was all just a nasty mind-game.

However, the homicide squad were faced with further problems in the investigation. Firstly, there was an increase in copycat murders, along with the usual extraordinary Los Angeles one-a-day murder rate; secondly, they faced a huge number of subsequently worthless tip-offs from the public. Every piece of information had to be checked out, just in case, no matter how unlikely it was thought to be, and that took up a colossal amount of police time; and thirdly, there were a huge number of false confessions, something which made the Dahlia murder such a complex and difficult case. Some of them appeared credible, while others were from people who clearly had mental issues. There was also a deluge of anonymous letters made up from newspaper and magazine clippings sent to the various Los Angeles newspaper offices, which didn't help matters either.

One such letter read: 'I will give up in Dahlia killing if I get 10 years. Don't try to find me'. That was received by the *Herald-Express*.

Apart from Robert 'Red' Manley, there have been many suspects and/ or persons of interest proposed as the unidentified killer of Elizabeth Short. Some have been unknown to the police while others have already been on their files.

There have been numerous investigations into the killing, as well as people claiming to know the identity of the Black Dahlia murderer. Those have most recently included Steve Hodel, who believed his late father, Dr George Hodel, was responsible, after finding pictures resembling Elizabeth Short at the back of one of his photo albums. He also later found that his father had been on the list of suspects in 1950 and police had bugged his home. However, the evidence appeared very flimsy and he was never charged.

I believe the most credible explanation is provided by Ms Piu Eatwell, who has worked as both a lawyer and a researcher for TV documentaries. She said in her recent book *Black Dahlia, Red Rose* that after being instructed by a rich Hollywood businessman, Mark Hansen, to get rid of her, Leslie Dillon, a 27-year-old drifter and bell worker, carried out the murder. Mark Hansen, originally from Denmark, had become a successful businessman by 1947, owning movie theatres and retaining part ownership of a nightclub. He was said to be possessive with women and had links to the Los Angeles underworld and the LAPD. He had a number of girls stay at a property in Carlos Avenue, of which Elizabeth Short was one, and he was said to be obsessed with her. However, he became frustrated with her when she would stay with him but not 'go all the way'. He was also ludicrously jealous when she had other boyfriends. Eventually, he tired of her and wanted to get rid of her, unfortunately choosing a psychopath to carry out the deed. And that man was Leslie Dillon. He was an alleged criminal and bootlegger, but worse still, he had psychopathic tendencies, which meant the murder was going to involve a horrifically gruesome mutilation.

But why was it so extreme and cruel?

It has been suggested that the killer had sexual inadequacies and that maybe Beth, being somewhat naive, inadvertently made some comment about that, thereby triggering the horrific torture and violence that resulted in her appalling death. It is surmised that after Leslie Dillon went too far in getting rid of her, placing Hansen, who had instigated the evil directive, in a very incriminating position, Hansen used his connections to hush up the investigation. Corruption was endemic in the LAPD at that time, and it appears that because of that, he succeeded in covering up his involvement. At least, that's the current theory amongst many.

Elizabeth Short was a beautiful young woman with little money. She was known to hang around with men for a free meal or ride home and had a carefree lifestyle. It was her modus operandi. She was basically a decent young woman who, at worst, was a bit of a freeloader. However, her portrayal in public slowly changed from innocent victim to a woman who went home with and 'entertained' lots of men. It was a terrible and inaccurate portrayal.

The media built up the notion that she was a free and easy girl who wouldn't take money for sex, but would allow men to pay for her on evenings out. Some reports were downright insensitive, if not underhand. One editor told a reporter to get hold of her mother and get the first interview. He said, 'Don't tell her that her daughter has been killed. Tell her she has won a beauty contest. Get all the background on her and her friends and then tell her she has been murdered and cut in two.'

With the editor breathing down his neck, that's exactly what the reporter did. And that's how the family were told. Anything for a good newspaper story. A bloody cruel approach in my view.

After the murder, Leslie Dillon allegedly contacted Dr Paul de River, the only forensic psychologist to be employed by the LAPD, initially offering to help find Elizabeth's killer, saying he wanted to hear his theories on the case because he had an interest in sexual psychopaths and sadism, and wanted to write a book about them.

When they spoke, Dillon apparently revealed details that only the murderer could know, such as the rose tattoo on Beth's thigh, which had been removed. In addition, he mentioned some facts about how the body had been mutilated, which the police had kept out of the public arena. And there was more.

After Elizabeth had been dropped off at the posh Biltmore Hotel, she was later seen at the more modest Aster Motel, where she, Mark Hansen and Leslie Dillon were allegedly seen by witnesses. On the cool morning of 15 January 1947, the day Beth's body was found in the vacant allotment, Henry Hoffman, the owner of the Aster Motel, was carrying out his rounds of the cabins. In cabin number 3, he made a horrifying discovery. The room was splattered with blood and there were faeces all over the bathroom and on the floor of the bedroom. But instead of reporting it to police, Hoffman, who had had a previous run-in with the law, namely for beating up his wife a few days earlier, just decided to clean up the mess, soaking and later burning the bloodstained sheets rather than risking becoming a person of interest.

However, the horror wasn't over. When he inspected cabin number 9, he found a bundle of women's clothes wrapped in brown paper. They were stained with blood. A further package of clothes containing a shoe and a bag, similar to those Elizabeth had been wearing, was found on a Los Angeles refuse dump a block from where Dillion lived. Those items were subsequently identified by Robert 'Red' Morley, who confirmed that they belonged to Elizabeth and that she was wearing them when they were travelling from San Diego to Los Angeles and onto the Biltmore Hotel six days before her mutilated body was found in the vacant allotment. In addition, witnesses reported seeing a black-haired girl there and a receipt for an extraordinarily large laundry bill was found at the motel after the killing. But thanks to Henry Hoffman, the LAPD continued to follow many useless leads and some very important evidence was destroyed. Curiously, the investigation into Leslie Dillon was suspended and subsequently ceased. Dr Paul de River believed Dillon murdered Beth Short, and he held that belief until the end of his life.

I have no reason to doubt his assertion, based on my own independent research. But, unbelievably, although he was a seasoned professional, he was harassed, subsequently losing his job, and he was also allegedly tailed by police cars. One of his daughters said she saw a police car following her to school. He also received a visit from a member of the police department telling him to keep quiet about the matter. He was later totally discredited. It was a sad end for a much lauded forensic psychologist.

Elizabeth Short reportedly befriended a lot of men while frequenting a fair number of nightclubs in Los Angeles, particularly while she was grieving for the death of the airman she had fallen in love with. Consequently, it became very difficult for police to determine whom she could have been with before she was murdered. Everyone was a suspect and they all needed to be checked out.

Los Angeles City grand jury took up the case in 1949 and they enquired specifically into whether the investigation had been mishandled and why Leslie Dillon had been let go. A report was filed at the end of the year when the jury reached the end of its term, to be replaced by a new team.

The report stated that the jury wanted the case to be investigated, but nothing more of value came out of it.

There was a lot of concern about young women in post-war America going to Hollywood and Los Angeles hoping they would be spotted by agents and eventually become stars, and the story of Elizabeth Short was presented as a warning to them by the media as to what could happen. Sadly, it came to represent the dangers and the dark side of Hollywood. Not great public relations.

And it is here that this tragic story of a young lady comes to a somewhat dubious end. In fairness to the LAPD, this disgusting crime did present them with an enormous task, but at the end of the day, justice wasn't delivered to the cruel and unknown but highly suspected perpetrator … and it probably never will be.

Master Sergeant Marcus Marymont. *Image:* Archive Photos

5.

Arsenic in the Air:
The Marcus Marymont Case

'Being betrayed by someone you love so much,
and thought you could trust wholeheartedly,
is the worst form of betrayal in life.'

Anon

Master Sergeant Marcus Marymont was a dapper airman stationed at the US Air Force base at Sculthorpe, Lincolnshire, in England, along with his wife, Helen Marymont, and their three children. He began a chance affair with a young woman, Cynthia Taylor, and rather than the expense of a divorce, he chose to use arsenic (trioxide) to gain his freedom to be with his new love.

I n February 1956, Cynthia Taylor was an attractive young woman, who had recently broken off with her husband of only six months. Unfortunately, two months later she found that she was pregnant, and spent most of her evenings knitting baby clothes and watching television.

In an effort to improve her life, her mother one evening in July 1956 suggested that they should go to a darts tournament at a local public house in Warren Row, outside Maidenhead. While sitting enjoying their drinks, two American airmen in civilian dress walked in and were introduced by the publican to Ms Taylor and her mother. One of the airmen was Master Sergeant Marcus Myron Marymont, who was with the 47th Bombardment Technical Wing at the US Air Force headquarters at Sculthorpe.

Cynthia Taylor was quite taken by the handsome airman, and readily

Cynthia Taylor.

accepted the offer to dance. They danced and enjoyed the evening together. Later, Ms Taylor and her mother declined an offer for a lift home, and so took a bus. However, the following night, Mr Marymont called around to her parents' home and asked her out for a date. Cynthia had other plans, but decided to join him and enjoyed the evening. They dated several more times, and a steady relationship soon became established. In October, Cynthia Taylor was admitted to hospital to have her child from her previous relationship. The child was a boy, and Mr Marymont came to visit mother and child in hospital. Despite the arrival of another man's baby, he admitted that he had fallen in love with her, and she felt the same about him. After her discharge from hospital, Mr Marymont and Ms Taylor began to date on a regular basis. He told her he was divorced and that his former wife was in North Carolina, USA, with their three children.

The affair continued and soon became a sexual relationship. Unfortunately for Ms Taylor, Mr Marymont's wife was actually living at the Sculthorpe air force base with their three children. It appears he was on 'temporary duty near London'. No real divorce appeared to be in sight.

In the meantime, Mrs Marymont had not been well for some time, and saw her doctor on a number of occasions for gastric upsets. Then, on 8 June1958 the Marymonts accepted a lunch invitation with some friends. It became apparent during the meal that Mrs Marymont was not well, and with apologies, her husband took her home. At home she fared little better, and after having rallied briefly from a gastric upset, her head fell backwards, her hands and lips started to turn blue and her eyes rolled back. She was clearly in a bad way and an ambulance was summoned.

At the air base hospital Mrs Marymont was placed under the care of (Dr) Captain Max Buchfuher. Unfortunately, by now Mrs Marymont's condition had worsened and she had become blue and appeared unconscious. Due to her desperate condition, she was placed into an oxygen tent. Unfortunately, despite the good doctor's efforts Helen Marymont died. Marcus Marymont took her passing very well, according to the doctor, 'He did not react very much at all, he was very calm.' In fact, he did an extraordinary thing: 'Doc, you did all you could.'

Helen Marymont.

He consoled the doctor!

Given Helen Marymont's history of gastric upsets, it appeared that an autopsy (post-mortem) was necessary. This was to be performed by Dr Albert Cook. Marcus Marymont was very unhappy with the idea of an autopsy. He mentioned that their children would not like the idea of their 'mother being cut up'. Dr Cook was adamant that it was necessary to find out why Helen Marymont died, given her medical history of gastric upsets.

An independent doctor, (Dr) Captain Ernest Courier, carried out a post-mortem of Mrs Marymont's body. He reached the conclusion that she had been poisoned by arsenic. However, he sought a second opinion through the Metropolitan Police Laboratory. As suspected, arsenic was found in her liver. In addition, her hair was analysed for the toxin.

Arsenic was found in three sections of her hair indicating three separate dosages. A heavy concentration was found at the roots of her hair indicating the fatal dose had entered her body some 24 hours earlier. Further along her hair, arsenic was again detected indicating another dose was ingested between a month and two months earlier. At 7–8 cm away from her hair roots, arsenic was again detected indicating another dose was taken about six months earlier. Helen Marymont had been chronically poisoned with arsenic.

Special agents carried out investigations into Marcus Marymont's activities and found further incriminating evidence, which included 69 letters received from Cynthia Taylor and that he also had access to arsenic at the University of Maryland laboratory at the base. There was also testimony from a chemist at Maidenhead, and there appeared sufficient evidence to prosecute Marcus Marymont for having poisoned his wife.

He was subsequently arrested and, on 8 September 1958, appeared before a court martial charged with murder and adultery (at that time adultery was an offence under the US Uniform Code of Military Justice). Marymont, not surprisingly, pleaded not guilty to both charges.

The prosecuting counsel said that Marymont decided to poison his wife with small doses of arsenic to give the impression of a chronic illness. The prosecution said any person who could carry out this crime had to be 'intelligent, cool and calculating'. 'If Marymont doesn't fit that description, no one does.'

The prosecution went on to describe how the poisoning had been carried out. 'He [Marymont] firstly tries a small dose of arsenic. It doesn't work. In May he tries another dose. It almost works, but she recovers from that. He waits until June and tries again. He goes to the hospital for some medicine and he dumps that dose of arsenic into her medicine. The medicine given to her to make her better, makes her worse.' The prosecution then declared, 'Murder was the only way out. Marymont was going to lose the woman he loved unless his wife was out of the way.'

Apparently, Marymont's marriage had already been shaky after his posting to Japan in 1954, prior to his meeting with Cynthia Taylor. In a statement released at court he said, 'Ours was a happy marriage until my return from Japan in 1954. I had been away for 18 months and when I returned I did not seem to have the same love and affection for my wife as before.'

Further, Mrs Marymont found a letter in his coat pocket that he had forgotten to post, which left no doubt in her mind that he husband was having an affair with Cynthia Taylor.

Cynthia Taylor also appeared in court where she gave evidence on the letters that were found in Marymont's room that confirmed their relationship.

Dr Nichols of the Metropolitan Police Laboratory, who carried out the second post-mortem of Helen Marymont, said that she had consumed more than the lethal dose of arsenic.

The defence, headed by Major William Karr, said that it had not been proved that Mrs Marymont's death was caused by her husband and went on to say, 'The probability of suicide or accident is just as great if not greater, than that of murder.'

The court was not impressed; however it took over five hours to reach a verdict. Marymont was eventually found guilty on both charges, and sentenced to hard labour for life. He was also dishonourably discharged from the United States Air Force with the loss of all benefits. A huge price, but it could have been his life.

Marymont appealed on several issues including the possibility of Helen Marymont suffering from a fatal illness (this was not supported by medical records). He eventually lost his appeal, and was transferred to the American federal prison in Kansas to serve out his sentence of life imprisonment with hard labour.

Maureen McLaughlin, who went missing and was found dead in 1992.

6.
A Dog and a Dame in a Ditch:
Who Murdered Maureen McLaughlin?

'When the fox hears the rabbit scream
he comes a-runnin', but not to help.'

Thomas Harris, *The Silence of the Lambs*

This was a mysterious case that was left over from when I worked at the Biological and Chemical Research Institute (BCRI) at Rydalmere in Sydney from 1987 to 1997. My colleague Dr Gary Levot was an extraordinary forensic entomologist who also carried out forensic work examining blowfly larvae to determine time of death of murder victims. This could have been a vital piece of evidence to solve this cold case, but for a snafu − 'a foul-up' of the samples submitted.

Mrs Wanda Steele was an avid bushwalker. Whenever the weather was suitable, she liked nothing better than a hike through some mountainous area or other. And so it was on 13 April 1992 when she set out looking for some wildflowers in the bush. Shortly before midday, she made her way along the State Mine Gully Road, a thoroughfare adjacent to the Blue Mountains National Park, enjoying her surroundings and the freedom of the wide-open space. As she walked, she saw something protruding out of the ground a little way in the distance. She didn't think any more about it until she drew level, when what she saw almost made her heave. It was a human arm and hand; the skin, infested with blowflies, peeling away from the flesh and bone. After taking a few minutes to recover her sensibilities, she immediately contacted the Lithgow police, who were soon on the scene.

Lithgow is a small town situated in the Central Tablelands of New South Wales. It was once a thriving coal mining area, but its glory days are well behind it, most people now recognising the place as an historical tourist destination. A two-hour drive west of Sydney, it nestles among several national parks, one of which is the Blue Mountains National Park, a World Heritage site.

The spot where Mrs Steele made her gruesome discovery was a favourite night-time parking haunt for local young people who cared little for the natural beauty of the area, despoiling it with all kinds of associated trash such as empty drink cans, used condoms, pieces of foil and even bongs.

The police team quickly donned protective clothing and secured the site before beginning the onerous task of clearing the debris that was lying on and around the immediate vicinity of the arm and hand. Having removed the rubbish, they started excavating the coarse river sand and stones that surrounded the protruding limb, proceeding slowly and carefully, as they were not sure whether the arm and hand were all there was or if they would find more body parts.

It wasn't a straightforward operation, as they started uncovering all kinds of scrap and detritus. Amongst the many finds were pieces of corrugated iron; a blue-coloured, 20-litre drum; a used automobile engine oil filter; an empty, clear plastic soft-drink bottle; four pieces of white PVC insulating tape; an empty, woven plastic sack, marked 'Pigeon Feed'; and a blue, floral patterned, ladies bolero, containing a bunch of keys in the left pocket and a brooch, in the shape of a marijuana leaf, attached to the front right.

The operation took quite some time, but they eventually accessed a body in its shallow grave. A cursory look revealed it to be that of an adult female. She was naked from the shoulders down, save for a white bra and a red-and-white skivvy. Her bra was fastened at the back and had been pulled up at the front, exposing her breasts. Further inspection showed a number of rings on the right hand and three earrings in the right earlobe, with a further earring under the left ear. At first glance, the head appeared to be resting on a piece of coarse carpet, but after the body had been lifted, it was found to be the rotting carcass of a dog, which when it was moved revealed two .22 calibre cartridges, both of them spent.

By the time the body had been recovered, photographs taken and exhibits meticulously detailed, night was falling, so the Lithgow Volunteer Rescue Association (LVRA) set up floodlighting so the work could continue. Shortly afterwards, Dr K. Fields, the government medical officer for the Lithgow district, arrived at the crime scene and examined the body, which was then transported to the Lithgow mortuary, where it was washed and examined externally by Dr Fields himself.

The most striking thing about the corpse was that it was decorated with numerous tattoos. Dr Fields duly photographed and recorded each one. There was an eight-point star on the inside left ankle, a rose with two faces on the left thigh, a marijuana leaf on the left buttock with the words 'Life be out of it', an angel on the right buttock, a stylised vulture sitting on a post with the words 'DEAD END 666' on the left upper arm, the word 'ARIES' and its symbol, along with the words 'Alice Cooper' with the symbol of a mouth and tongue on the right thigh, and tattoos of hinges on both inner elbows. She had clearly been a young woman with attitude.

Finally, a set of fingerprints was taken for identification purposes before the body was encased in a body bag, which was then fastened and placed into a sealed refrigerator to await its final trip to the Sydney City Mortuary in Glebe the following morning.

The body was identified as that of Maureen Ann McLaughlin, but the presence of the dead dog and the two spent .22 calibre cartridges were a real puzzler. What was their significance to Ms McLaughlin's death?

The dog was identified as a Rottweiler-kelpie cross and traced to its owner, Ceanne Gwendoline Towers. The case detectives were dispatched to interview her, discovering that Ceanne had been in a long-term relationship with a woodchopper, Graham 'Chook' Fowler, who allegedly dealt cannabis to supplement his income. The couple had two children and Sheba, the Rottweiler-kelpie. Further enquiries showed that Fowler was a man with a history of violence, and he'd often engaged in both physical and mental aggression against Ceanne. On one occasion, during a domestic argument, he'd armed himself with a kitchen knife and tried to stab her, but the knife had struck the kitchen table and deflected into his wrist.

He'd also been violent to his ex-wife, and there was a story going round that he'd once thrown a woman from his car while it was still moving, causing serious injuries. Like many people, his aggressive attitude intensified after he'd been drinking.

The incident that led to the death of Ceanne's Rottweiler-kelpie occurred after Fowler flipped over the dog digging holes in the rear yard of their home. On 14 December 1991, he took a .22 calibre semiautomatic rifle out of a cupboard, put the dog into a ute and drove to Newnes Drift (State Mine Gully), an area he knew well from his work, killing the dog with two shots to the head.

Meanwhile, Ceanne had rung the Lithgow police, fearing for the dog's safety, but she was too late. Fowler returned home and admitted to what he'd done, whereupon a distressed and tearful Ceanne contacted her mother and father, telling them what had happened. The three of them went to search Newnes Drift and found Sheba's body. Ceanne's father then took a pick and shovel out of his vehicle and dug a deep grave in which to place the body. When they finished the burial, Ceanne marked the site with a pink beaded white-plastic cross.

At the same time as the police were chasing up the possible dog connection, the post-mortem into Maureen McLaughlin took place. The morning after her body had been discovered, it was collected from the Lithgow mortuary and driven to the Glebe Department of Forensic Medicine, where it was formally identified by its fingerprints and Maureen's distraught parents.

The post-mortem, carried out by forensic pathologist Dr Lillian Schwartz, revealed a number of injuries to Maureen's body, and a sample of maggots (*Calliphora stygia* larvae) was taken to be analysed in order to provide an estimate of the time of death. Unfortunately, owing to a snafu before arrival at the BCRI entomology laboratory, it wasn't possible. In addition, a number of swabs, smears and specimens were collected and delivered to the Department of Forensic Medicine.

Dr Schwartz concluded that although the decompositional changes of the deceased suggested a period of approximately seven to 14 days after death, and some of the injuries seen on the body might have been caused after death, the large number of head injuries and bruises seen on the body strongly suggested that Maureen had died as a result of the head injuries.

An analysis of body tissues (taken because a suitable blood sample was not available) revealed that there was nordiazepam 0.42 milligrams per kilogram present in Maureen's liver and 0.01 milligrams per kilogram of the same substance in her stomach. I concluded that at those levels the drug was not responsible for her death, and although the spleen and muscle samples contained small amounts of alcohol, that was most likely due to the fermentation of glucose in the body from bacteria and/or yeast during decomposition.

A later post-mortem confirmed the findings of Dr Schwartz that the evidence of head trauma and possible strangulation indicators were the probable causes contributing to Maureen's death. And so it was on to the inquest to determine the circumstances surrounding it. It took place on 6 July 1993 at Lithgow Coroner's Court, before the coroner, Mr Derek Hand.

Members of Maureen's family and some acquaintances came forward in an effort to shed some light on the matter, but other than evidence that she'd been a heavy smoker and that, unusually for her, she'd left her boxes of cigarettes in her flat on the night of her disappearance, scant progress was made towards solving the mystery, and after two days, the court was unable to reach any sort of conclusion. However, the coroner did comment on the coincidence of Graham Fowler shooting his de facto's dog and the fact that Maureen's body had been found where the dog had been buried. He was, though, quite satisfied that that was all it was, and that there was nothing to connect Fowler and Ceanne with Maureen, and that it was all just an extreme coincidence.

Unable to determine either the manner or cause of Maureen's death, the coroner returned an open verdict, meaning the case remained open, but with no nominated person of interest.

A reward of $100,000 was offered for information, but met with no response, so when the Western Region Unsolved Homicide Team (WRUHT) renewed its investigation into the case, designating it Strike Force Checkley, in September 2009, it was increased to $200,000. At the time of writing this story, the reward money is still available, so if you have any information that may help investigators to close this cold case and bring the perpetrator(s) to justice, please call Crime Stoppers on 1800 333 000.

7.
A Cry in the Night:
A Misplaced Love

'Nobody ever forgets where he buried a hatchet.'
Kim Hubbard

The cold, bleak evening of Saturday 10 June 2000, in the quiet rural town of Uralla, didn't promise anything out of the ordinary. And why would it? The last piece of real excitement seen in the sleepy hilly area in the Northern Tablelands of the New England region of New South Wales had taken place some 130 years earlier when Frederick Ward, aka Captain Thunderbolt, the notorious bushranger, had been shot by the police on 25 May 1870. Situated halfway between Brisbane and Sydney, the 2300 who inhabited the town went quietly about their business, totally unconcerned with the world outside. But that tranquillity was about to be disturbed.

At 8.40 pm, the phone in the local police station rang. The caller said, 'I'm from Queen Street. There's some sort of commotion going on at the flats next door. Could you come and check it out?'

A police unit went to investigate and found Marion Read (often called Mary) and a young female companion shivering outside a flat. Leo Hunt, also known as Snow because of his pure white hair, was standing inside, by the sliding glass door. The police ushered Marion back into the flat.

'What's going on?' one of the police officers asked.

'Snow assaulted me,' Marion replied.

Further conversation ascertained that both parties had been drinking, something that had made for an uneasy relationship between the two in the past. Then Marion said, 'Snow's accusing me of having an affair with the bloke in flat four, but I don't even know him.'

The police officer looked from Marion to a scowling Snow and back again. 'Jealous, is he?'

Marion nodded. 'And possessive.'

'So what happened tonight?'

Uralla Police Station, NSW. *Source:* Detective Sergeant Barry Fay (NSWPF retired)

Marion fixed Snow with a glare. 'He knocked me glasses off me face and forced me up to that bloke's flat, screaming at me. He kicked me and knocked me glasses off me head. I don't even know the bloke in flat four.'

'If you get another AVO,' Snow snarled, 'you're dead. I'll fucking kill you.'

'I didn't get the last AVO,' Marion retorted, 'the police did. And for your information, I didn't call them tonight.'

The police officer had heard enough. 'Get up, Snow, and wait outside,' he said. Then he turned to Marion. 'Based on what you've told me, I'm going to charge him with assault. I'll be back in a moment.'

An AVO was applied for and subsequently issued by an after-hours magistrate in Parramatta. Its terms were read to Hunt. 'Do you understand all the conditions about not going near Mary?' the police officer asked.

'Yeah, yeah, I understand,' Hunt replied. 'All this for a fucking gin!'

At five minutes to midnight, Snow was conditionally bailed not to approach Marion, who had been strongly warned by the police that she should lock herself in after they left. Unfortunately, she failed to take their advice and, shortly after midnight, there came a knock at her door. Foolishly, Marion opened it. It was Hunt. He forced her back into the flat, but she managed to evade him, turn, and run outside. Hunt picked up a carving knife from the kitchen and gave chase. He was intent on carrying out his earlier threat. Marion ran towards the caravan park, but Hunt was faster and stronger, and he soon caught up with her.

Just 40 minutes after he'd been issued with the AVO, witnesses from the nearby caravan park heard a couple of short, bloodcurdling screams as Hunt stabbed Marion repeatedly in the back before running off, leaving the carving knife embedded where he'd made his last frenzied thrust.

A few minutes later, the police emergency line received a triple-O call. The caller asked to speak to the Uralla police.

'I can't put you through, sir,' the operator replied, 'but I can get them to come and see you.'

A short silence followed.

'Hello?' the operator said, checking to see if the caller was still on the line.

The caller repeated his request, and the operator repeated what she'd said, adding, 'Or I can get them to contact you by phone?'

The caller then asked the operator to contact the police for him.

'Okay,' she replied. 'What's your name?'

'Snow Hunt.'

'I'm sorry,' the operator said, 'what's your name?'

'Hunt.' Snow also gave his telephone number.

'Can I say what this is regarding, Mr Hunt?' the operator asked.

'What's that?'

'What is it regarding?'

'I wanna talk to the police.'

'Okay,' the operator replied. 'You don't have an emergency that you need the police to attend to straight away?'

'I think so, yes,' Hunt said.

'You do need the police there straight away?' the operator queried, in an effort to confirm what help was being sought.

'Yes, yes please,' Hunt replied.

'Well, it's quicker if you give me the details …'

At that point, Hunt terminated the call.

About 15 minutes later, the Uralla police were contacted. They arrived at Hunt's residence at just gone one o'clock in the morning. The house was in darkness and the front door was closed. A police officer rapped on it sharply, calling out, 'Snow are you in there? What's going on?'

The door opened and Hunt slowly emerged from the darkness. 'What the …?'

'What's going on? Why did you call the cops, talking about Marion?' the police officer asked.

'You obviously dunno what's happened,' Hunt replied.

'Where's Mary?'

There was no answer forthcoming, so the police officer repeated his question in a slightly more assertive manner. Hunt stood there for a few moments, but eventually answered, 'In the park.'

'Where in the park?

'In the caravan park.'

'What have you done to her?'

Hunt stood motionless, saying nothing, but after a few minutes and some further discussion, he led the police to the scene of the crime, where he pointed towards a prone body. 'There she is,' he said.

Marion was lying face down in the grass, a large amount of blood around her nose and mouth area, and a large-handled kitchen knife protruding from her back, just as Hunt had left her. A police officer turned to him in despair and anger. 'What have you done?'

'I've had two packets of Serepax [a brand of oxazepam] and I don't know what I've done,' came the reply.

'Where did you get the knife?' the police officer asked.

Hunt shrugged. 'What knife? I don't know.'

The police officer then placed Hunt under arrest before cautioning him and putting him in the police car. Then he radioed for back-up. Shortly after, more police and an ambulance arrived at what had been declared to be a crime scene. The ambulance officer who checked the deceased for any signs of life was also asked to check Hunt because he'd said that he'd taken two packets of Serepax, but the police that had come with the ambulance said that Hunt should go to the hospital, so he was taken out of the police car and handcuffed before being escorted to the ambulance, which took him to Armidale Hospital, some 23 kilometres away.

In the meantime, the area around the corpse was preserved until crime scene and police detectives arrived, and a search was made of Hunt's premises. Two empty blister packs of Serepax were found. A government contractor showed up at about 7.30 am and transported Marion's body to Armidale Hospital, where she was formally pronounced dead.

The ambulance transporting Hunt to the accident and emergency section of the hospital arrived at a couple of minutes before two o'clock. The police officers accompanying him reported that he appeared to be alert and orientated, and that there were no other evident problems.

The doctor on duty was briefed on what had happened, and when asked for his version of events, Hunt just said, 'I warned her.'

While hooking Hunt up to a monitor to check his cardiac and

respiratory systems, the nursing staff asked the police officer if the handcuffs were really necessary because they were making the task more difficult. By way of an answer, the officer told them that Hunt was alleged to have murdered someone earlier in the evening and that he had taken two foil packs of Serepax.

It was decided to treat him for a drug overdose. Part of the treatment involved the administration of charcoal to absorb the poisons, but Hunt was unhappy with that and objected, saying, 'Do I have to have this shit?'

'Sorry, you have to have it,' the nurse replied, matter-of-factly.

Further assessments were also carried out, including the Glasgow Coma Scale (GCS), a test to determine how alert a person is, with a score of 15 being totally normal. Hunt was assessed as 14, and the testing nurse reported that the only area that Hunt seemed confused about was where he was. As far as the nursing staff was concerned, the result of the test showed the oxazepam he had apparently ingested was having a minimal effect at that time, so they asked him what he had taken.

'Two packets of Serepax,' Hunt replied.

It was clear from his breath that he'd been drinking, so after a few hours, another GCS was performed, but on that occasion, there was no response to speech or spontaneous action. Judging him to no longer be a threat, Hunt's handcuffs were removed. However, after a final test involving a sternal rub, he awoke and started to throw his arms around, swinging punches at nursing staff, so he had to be re-handcuffed. At the same time he started to verbally abuse the nurses, saying things such as, 'What the fuck are you doing?'

A further GCS, carried out an hour and a half later at 6 am, rated him as a 10, and he only responded to the sternal rub. Once again, he was released from his handcuffs, but when a nurse attempted to aid his respiration, he suddenly propped himself up on his elbow and said, 'I'm going to kill you,' at the same time taking a swing at her. She screamed and colleagues came rushing to her aid, re-handcuffing Hunt once more. It took him an hour to settle down. It was discovered later that he'd developed a tolerance to the oxazepam and had apparently been taking it for many years in an attempt to keep himself calm. Of course, any alcohol in his system would have exacerbated the effects.

Five hours later, at midday, a blood sample was taken. It was found to contain oxazepam 2.2 milligrams per litre (mg/L), which is more than eight times higher than the therapeutic range (0.09 to 0.44 mg/L, average 0.265 mg/L). However, there was no trace of alcohol, even though a witness had said Hunt had smelt strongly of alcohol and had been half drunk. But on the other hand, the witness had also said that Hunt had been talking normally and had no problems standing up or walking.

Such apparent contradictions can be explained by the time interval between Hunt drinking and having his blood tested (it's probable that any alcohol would have been metabolised to undetectable levels) and Hunt being a regular drinker (he would have been more tolerant of alcohol and able to metabolise it faster than someone who drank infrequently or just on social occasions).

Marion Reid's post-mortem indicated that she'd had a rough life, with several health problems and a number of bruises of varying ages being revealed. The wounds that most likely took her life were apparent in her chest, and defensive injuries to her hands showed she'd desperately tried to prevent her untimely demise.

Leo 'Snow' Hunt stood trial on 12 November 2001, some 17 months after Marion Reid had been killed. The trial took place in the NSW Supreme Court in Tamworth, where Hunt was charged with his de facto's murder.

I attended Tamworth Court for the committal hearing and gave evidence to do with the level of oxazepam found in Hunt's blood. I was cross-examined on a number of issues relating to the drug, including tolerance, absorption time and how long it takes for its effects to become apparent with regard to the quantity taken. For example, if 50 Serepax tablets were taken at one sitting, how would that manifest itself in the stomach?

My answer was that such a large number of tablets would clump together and form a bolus in the stomach and be absorbed over time, the exact length of which would depend on whether food was present. Further questions addressed the possibility that oxazepam ingestion can produce a paradoxical reaction of acute rage rather than sedation. For example, I was asked that from what I knew of the case, and based on my knowledge generally, if one of the paradoxical reactions such as acute rage, stimulation or excitement were to occur, would anything make it possible for that reaction to occur within, say, 15 minutes of a large overdose of tablets having been taken.

I replied, 'Fifteen minutes seems a bit too fast for me. It would have to be at least a minimum of half an hour. You have to allow time for the stomach to actually absorb the drug into the bloodstream, and you would be still looking at half an hour to an hour for the effects to actually to come into play.'

Both prosecution and defence counsels were basically trying to establish when Hunt took the drug overdose. Was it before or after the murder?

It seemed to me that it was more likely Hunt had taken the drug overdose after the murder, possibly in an attempt to take his own life as well. However, even if the drug overdose had been taken just before the murder (and there seemed to be no motivation for that), there had been insufficient time for the drug to manifest the various effects put to me, paradoxical or otherwise. That conclusion was borne out by other witness evidence that followed my toxicological evidence.

Hunt was found guilty as charged and sentenced to a minimum of 20 years imprisonment. Given that he was 68-years-old at the time of sentencing, it seems likely he'll spend the rest of his life in jail, while some folk in Uralla will forever be haunted by Marion's agonising cry in the night for as long as they live.

8.

Affairs of the Heart and Poison:

Almost a Victim

'If you drink much from a bottle marked "poison"
it is certain to disagree with you sooner or later.'

Lewis Carroll, *Alice's Adventures in Wonderland*

The vast majority of poisoning cases with which I was involved and provided expert advice/evidence for at local, district and supreme court levels dealt mostly with the more common drugs. For example, stimulants such as MDMA (ecstasy), methamphetamine, amphetamine, ephedrine, phentermine, and central nervous system (CNS) depressants such as morphine, heroin, benzodiazepines (diazepam, oxazepam etc.), cannabis, methadone and, of course, alcohol. However, from time to time, unusual poisons appeared in my casework. One such case involved a pesticide rather than drugs.

Back in 2001, a married couple in a small country town were going through some marital difficulties and the bored farmer's wife embarked on a number of affairs. What had started out as a passionate romance with her 'wild man' soon soured as the dreary reality of marital duties and farm life set in. But country towns being what they are, word soon reached her husband, and when he discovered her most recent liaison, he decided that enough was enough and plotted to murder her.

Being a farmer, he'd had occasion to kill foxes that had threatened his livestock with the potent pesticide Phosdrin, and still having plenty of it in one of his sheds, he determined that would be ideal for what he had in mind. The only problem was how to administer it without his wife noticing. Fortunately for the farmer, she was into natural therapy products, a form of homeopathy, and took colloidal silver (believed to be a naturopathic treatment for asthma) every day, so on the morning of 20 May, the farmer added half a millilitre of Phosdrin to her colloidal silver and waited for the inevitable.

However, things didn't go according to plan.

His wife took one sip of the colloidal silver and was immediately alerted to its foul and different taste. She spat out what was in her mouth and rinsed with cold water, but couldn't avoid swallowing a small amount. Later on, she felt woozy, was unable to focus properly, was shaking badly, had no control over her bowels and threw up violently over the toilet floor. Somehow, she managed to call for an ambulance. When it arrived, she was sitting in a chair, sobbing. The paramedics asked her what had happened, to which she replied, 'My husband's poisoned me.' She was rushed to hospital, where she recovered, having more or less saved her own life through her prompt actions of spitting and rinsing and subsequent involuntary vomiting.

The treating doctor took a blood sample, which was examined for the presence of mevinphos (Phosdrin), but none was detected. However, a search of the farm turned up a bottle of red liquid marked Phosdrin, which contained mevinphos, as did the colloidal silver medication. Mevinphos was also detected in a drinking glass and in the vomit-stained towel taken from the toilet.

No matter how it's administered, mevinphos is a highly toxic organophosphorus insecticide. It affects the central nervous system and the eyes, and its action is direct and quick. Toxic effects include nausea, vomiting, diarrhoea, abdominal cramps, headache, dizziness, blurred vision, salivation, sweating and confusion, and they can appear within 15 minutes to two hours after exposure. It was developed from a nerve gas program during the Second World War, and along with its close cousins (various chemical analogues) is designed to kill – and kill very effectively.

The husband was initially charged with attempted murder, but when the matter went to trial, some legal wrangling saw the charge reduced to administering poison with intent to injure. However, in an unbelievable turn of events, the wife became the defence's star witness by changing her evidence, or as the police termed it, she 'did a backflip in the witness box'.

This is part of what she said: 'I felt that he only did it to frighten me. He could probably have cut my throat, or he could have given me a whole heap, and given me a cup of tea. Phosdrin works within three seconds.' (Note: Not even deadly cyanide works that fast.)

I wasn't called to give expert testimony and let the court know just how close to death the farmer's wife had come, but when I spoke to the Department of Public Prosecutions and asked what sentence would be appropriate for an offence of that nature, they indicated at least a period of jail time.

In the event, the farmer was given just 250 hours of community service. Not bad for attempted murder – which most likely could have succeeded but for the victim's effective bodily functions.

9.

The Case of the One-Armed Would-Be Rapist

'First you take a drink,
then the drink takes a drink,
then the drink takes you.'

F. Scott Fitzgerald

Because of its easy availability, alcohol is the drug most commonly associated with sexual assault cases. It's rapidly absorbed into the bloodstream after ingestion and distributes throughout the entire body, including, most importantly, the central nervous system (CNS), where its depressant effects are the most profound. In drug-facilitated sexual assault cases, the victims quite often consume the alcohol voluntarily, particularly when the perpetrator provides the alcoholic beverage in copious quantities to the potential victim. Alcohol decreases inhibitions, impairs perception and may cause loss of consciousness and/or amnesia, especially when other CNS drugs, such as diazepam, are used.

On the cool evening of 12 July 2006, Sandra Clooney met up with Ken Grose for a social drink at the Five Dock Hotel. Ken had had a hard life, having lost an arm in an industrial accident, and he was keen to get back on the social scene. The couple chatted away quite amicably, and throughout the evening Ken kept Sandra well supplied with drinks, ranging from VBs (Victoria Bitter beers) to Sambuca (an anise-flavoured liqueur). Perhaps unsurprisingly, Sandra started to be affected by the alcohol, becoming quite light-headed as well as exhibiting some more obvious outward signs such as uttering the occasional slurred word and becoming more voluble. Ken wasn't slow in noticing the deterioration and thought it was going to be his lucky night. The real giveaway was when Sandra said, 'Go ... osh, I feel quite pissed, Ken.'

Being nothing if not a 'gentleman', Ken went up to the bar and ordered more drinks, saying to the staff, 'I'm going to get a root [have sex] tonight.'

The extra drinks weren't really necessary, given what Ken Grose had in mind, because by the time he got back to the table, he could see Sandra was well under the weather and quite incapable of getting herself home. Leaving the drinks, he took her outside and she got into his vehicle, thinking that Ken was going to drive her home. However, he had another idea in mind. As he drove, Sandra dozed off. She was obviously far gone and Ken had drunk enough to be emboldened to act out his fantasy.

He pulled over, stopped his motor vehicle, opened the door and dragged Sandra out, both of them spilling into the gutter alongside the road. Sandra didn't stir, so he undid her jeans and pulled both them and her panties down before unzipping the fly of his pants.

Unfortunately for Ken, things were not about to go to plan, and a police officer on his way back to the station after dealing with another matter at the nearby Western Suburbs Soccer Club noticed them. He went back to the club and asked the manager and doorman of the club to accompany him as witnesses. When they returned, Sandra was lying face down on the roadway, her jeans and panties down to her knees, with Ken on top of her, moving his pelvis slowly up and down over her exposed bottom.

'Hey, what's going on here?' the officer asked.

Ken stood up, revealing the fly of his pants was undone. Sandra, being unconscious, remained where she was.

A comatose Sandra was placed in the police car and driven to the hospital, while Ken was taken to the police station and charged with attempted sexual assault. When Sandra regained consciousness, she didn't have a clue where she was and was totally unaware of what had happened to her. She was subjected to testing, involving a sexual assault investigation kit, in which blood and urine samples were taken. The samples were then forwarded to an accredited laboratory for analysis.

A blood sample taken the following day, at 12 o'clock, 10 hours after Sandra and Ken had been taken in by the police, was found to contain ecstasy or 3, 4-Methylenedioxymethylamphetamine (MDMA) 0.10 milligrams per litre, pseudoephedrine 0.05 milligrams per litre (possibly, an impurity in the MDMA preparation), diazepam less than 0.1 milligrams per litre, nordiazepam less than 0.1 milligrams per litre, and more significantly, alcohol 0.125 grams per 100 millilitres (decilitre) of blood. The diazepam and nordiazepam readings indicated that a drug such as Valium had been taken sometime earlier.

When asked what her blood alcohol level would have been at 2 am, about the time Sandra and Ken were caught in the act, I said that the lowest possible reading would have been 0.225 grams per decilitre of blood and the highest reading 0.375 grams, with a more probable reading of 0.325 grams. While Sandra was a seasoned drinker of alcohol (and she apparently had a problem in that area), they were very high readings, which alone would have accounted for her condition (as observed by witnesses and police) before even taking the other drugs detected in her blood into account. Consequently, her ability to ward off Ken's unwanted sexual advances was severely compromised.

The matter ended up in court, where the magistrate found that the prosecution had failed to produce enough evidence that Ken had attempted to rape Sandra, as penile penetration appeared not to have occurred. Ken was cleared and the case was dismissed.

As one wag was overheard saying on leaving the court, 'Yeah, he was armless but not 'armless!'

Well, this potential rapist was very lucky.

10.

The Lady in the Bath Water:

Death of an 'Angel of Mercy'

'Chains of habit are too light to be felt
until they are too heavy to be broken.'

Warren Buffett

Propofol (2, 6-diisopropylphenol) is a short-acting intravenous anaesthetic drug used as a preoperative treatment in hospitals. It's available
under the trade name of Diprivan and is a sedative-hypnotic which is
used as an intravenous anaesthetic agent. It's available as an oil/water
emulsion in 20–100 ml vials that contain 10 mg/ml as the free acid.

Abuse of propofol appears to be rare, although it featured in the
death of the American singer Michael Jackson on 25 June 2009. The
Los Angeles County Coroner ruled that he'd suffered acute propofol
intoxication, although a sedative (lorazepam or Ativan) was also a
contributory factor.

Propofol's use is characterised by a quick onset of action, a short
duration of activity, and a dose-dependent depth of sedation. That
means the depth of anaesthesia can be induced according to the dosage
given to the patient. It's well known that propofol administration, even

as a therapeutic dose, can cause respiratory depression, so oxygen and respiratory assistance is generally needed, with its use being more appropriate in a hospital setting, where such facilities are available.

Propofol has gained a reputation of being a popular recreational drug, particularly amongst young health care professionals who have ready access to it, because of the euphoria, hallucinations and disinhibitions that have been observed with propofol anaesthesia. One female radiographer even described the preparation as 'the milk of human kindness' before the drug, ironically, took her life. And that's not the only recorded tragedy.

D octor Linda Goodhart was a well-respected anaesthetist. She was very professional and highly regarded by her colleagues and assisting nurses. She'd recently passed her fellowship in anaesthetics and was on her way to becoming a consultant – the pinnacle of her career – and she was still only in her thirties. Linda was a 'social animal' and had many friends in Sydney, although most were doctors and various other professionals. Despite her physical attractiveness, she had a troubled love life and her boyfriends treated her poorly.

Sadly, she was attracted to 'bad boys'. Another moth to a flame.

One in particular, Dan, a regular visitor to her apartment, was into drugs and violence, and on one occasion he caused an injury to her face. She texted him later to say, 'My whole eye and cheekbone is bruised and I'm seeing double.' Her relationship with him appeared to be mainly based on sex and drugs (such as cannabis and cocaine). That Dan didn't value her as she deserved and treated her badly was obvious to all and sundry, and her friends urged her to get out of the relationship. But to further complicate things, Linda was also having an affair with another doctor at the same time, which caused her a lot of emotional pain during their time together. The other doctor was in a de facto relationship and was even with Linda the weekend before he got married. What a tangled web we weave!

Nevertheless, Dr Goodhart didn't allow the complications of her love life to interfere with her work, always performing her duties well, exhibiting great clinical skills and showing great empathy towards her patients. But on the morning of 18 June 2006, that was all to change.

She was rostered on as the emergency obstetric anaesthetic registrar, but failed to show. At first, it was assumed she'd been held up in traffic or by some other minor inconvenience, but as the morning wore on and she failed to respond to phone and page calls, her colleagues started to grow concerned. At 10.30 am, the switchboard advised Dr Howard, another anaesthetic senior registrar, that she hadn't arrived at work for her 8 am start and inquired if he knew where she was. 'This is so out of character for her not to show up for work without calling,' he said. He then attempted to call her on her mobile and landline without success, at which point the consultant anaesthetist asked him to go to her apartment to check everything was okay. He arrived at about 11 am, but was unable to gain entry, so he sought out the security manager for the apartments and expressed his concern for Linda's welfare. Understanding his anxiety, the manager phoned for a locksmith, who arrived at 11.45 am and succeeded in gaining entry to the modest one-bedroom apartment.

Apart from the bedroom, it contained a separate bathroom and an open area living room with a connecting kitchen and adjoining exterior balcony. As the three men entered, they passed blood stains on the tiled floor outside the bathroom, near an unplugged television set. The bathroom door was ajar. They went in, hearts in mouths, and found Linda Goodhart's naked body lying in a foetal position, partially submerged, in the bathtub. Inserted in her arm was an intravenous cannula with a syringe attached, which was gently floating in the bath water.

The locksmith immediately rang for the police and an ambulance. When the police arrived, they established a crime scene and took brief statements from the three men. The CSI (crime scene investigation) team then examined the area and photographed various items.

On one corner of the bath, there were four green candle holders, each containing a burnt-out candle, and there was black sooting on the tiles above. In a nearby bin, they located a black mobile phone and an empty vial of Diprivan (a brand of propofol). Wrappings and medical paraphernalia were found throughout the apartment, as were copious supplies of Diprivan.

The quantity of Diprivan found posed the question: Did she commit suicide or was it an accident caused by recreational use that had gone terribly wrong?

After her body had been conveyed by government contractors to the local hospital for death certification, police carried out a further inspection of the apartment, finding two more vials of Diprivan in a toiletries bag in her bedroom cupboard, along with two vibrators and condoms. As propofol can be used to induce and enhance sexual pleasure, it suggested that the supplies were for recreational use and that Linda's death had been accidental.

A blood sample taken from Linda's body at the post-mortem was found to have present propofol 2.6 milligrams per litre. Her urine sample was found to have present 0.8 milligrams of propofol and her bile sample 3 milligrams per litre of propofol.

For the induction of anaesthesia, blood levels of between 6–10 milligrams per litre are necessary, but during maintenance of anaesthesia, levels of about 2–4 mg/L are sufficient. The level of propofol found in Linda's blood was within this latter range, and the presence of modest levels of the drug in her urine and bile indicated she was alive for some time before she became immersed in the bath water. Therefore, it was concluded that assisted death or murder was unlikely. That reasoning was further backed up by the number of needle marks on her body, which suggested regular usage of the drug.

The risk of death due to self-administered propofol intoxication is low, mainly due to the low concentration found in commercial vials (20 ml containing 200 mg propofol or 500mg/50 ml in a pre-filled syringe). That's equivalent to a standard dose of 2–2.5 mg/kg body weight for the induction of general anaesthesia. The fast-acting narcotic effect of propofol (one to two minutes after injection) prevents self-injection of more than one vial at a time. Linda Goodhart would have been well aware of that, although healthcare workers, such as medical and nursing staff, who have easier access to the drug, have a greater potential for addiction, and deaths have occurred through over dosage.

The number of vials of propofol found in Dr Goodhart's apartment gave rise to the reasonable assumption that she had used the drug regularly and enjoyed its effects, thereby developing some degree of tolerance. And given her stressed environment, it may well have been her only way of achieving some degree of emotional and sexual fulfilment.

On the night of her untimely death, it's very likely that she'd returned from a difficult hospital shift and was seeking some physical and mental relief. After some attempts at inserting the cannula (hence the blood stains in the hallway), she slipped out of her clothes and into a warm bath (having previously lit the candles for mood) to relax and enjoy the effects of the drug. It was probably something she'd done on many previous occasions with no problem, but, unfortunately, that night was going to be quite different. Her fatigue from work may have been worse than usual and, as she rested, she drifted off to sleep and her head slipped beneath the bath water. Blissfully unaware, she would have been asleep as she drowned.

In his report, the pathologist wrote, 'The presence of pulmonary oedema and generalised organ congestion is consistent with both administration of an overdose of a respiratory depressant agent and death due to immersion.'

I said in my evidence to the Corner's Court that it would appear that the propofol was self-administered, probably recreationally, resulting in respiratory depression and consequent anoxia with the possibility of immersion resulting in her death. I had to agree with the pathologist that death was due to immersion, essentially drowning. However, I also opined that the level of propofol present in her blood, in an apparently tolerant person, did not appear to be excessive, though quite sufficient to result in central nervous system depression.

It's an unfortunate trait of humans to resort to substance abuse to relieve stress from overwork and/or poor relationships, sexual or otherwise. A subsequent inquest found that Dr Linda Goodhart's was an accidental death with propofol a contributory factor in the snuffing out of a promising young medical professional's life, just like the flames of the candles found in her bathroom.

As Sir Elton John so eloquently put it in his song about the death of Marilyn Monroe, a young movie legend of comparable age, 'she lived her life like a candle in the wind ...'

And so it appeared, did the good doctor. A terrible loss to the medical profession.

11.
A Bad Night at the Tavern:
Who killed Tiffany Graham?

'Nothing is a matter of life and death,
except life and death.'

Angela Carter

MDMA (or 3, 4-Methylenedioxymethamphetamine) has no approved medical use in Australia, but because of its stimulant and hallucinogenic effects, it's become a popular drug of abuse among adolescents and young adults who attend rave or rock parties. It's probably best known as ecstasy, although it has other street names, such as XTC, ADAM and Vitamin E. MDMA is a ring-substituted derivative of phenethylamine, which has close structural features related to both amphetamines and hallucinogens, such as mescaline.

The usual method of ingestion is via the mouth, in tablet form, which enables rapid absorption, although injection has been reported as having the quickest onset and producing a more intense but shorter lived experience. Two other common methods of taking MDMA are via the nose (snorting) and as a suppository.

The onset of action is usually within 30 to 40 minutes and a maximal response is achieved in about one or two hours. The duration of action is about four to six hours (average five hours) and the drug and its metabolites are excreted mainly in the urine.

The negative effects of ecstasy are dose-related, in that their severity is correlated with both the total number of doses consumed and the frequency of usage. The effect of taking larger doses has been reported as being mainly hallucinatory, with undesirable side effects increasing in line with the amount taken. Short-term high-dose usage of MDMA has produced incidences of hyperthermia (elevated body temperature) and, in some cases, severe hyponatremia (abnormally low concentration of salt in the blood), which is generally unresponsive to medical intervention by the time the victim reaches appropriate care, resulting in the death of that person.

Just after midnight on 25 January 2003, Tiffany ('Tiff') Graham and her friend Shaun Brooks ('Brooksy'), were in the Wollongong mall, where they met up with some friends, Ryan Chapman, Dean Jones (a former boyfriend of Tiffany) and Jay Hornsey. They then went to Cooney's Tavern in Keira Street, Wollongong, where they gravitated to the upper level.

Cooney's Tavern is a popular nightclub and pub, and everyone appeared to be in a good spirits, keen to enjoy themselves, socialise and listen to the music.

Ryan Chapman was really getting into the festive mood. 'I need a drink,' he said. 'Do any of you guys want one?'

A shaking of heads indicated the others were okay, so he headed downstairs to the bar. While he was walking through the crowd, he was approached by a stranger of foreign appearance

'Hey, mate, you want some pills or a pill?'

'Yeah, okay,' Chapman said. 'I'll take one.'

The stranger then reached into his pocket and pulled out some light-grey tablets.

Cooney's Tavern, Keira Street, Wollongong.

'That'll be 30 dollars,' he said, giving Chapman one of them.

Chapman handed over three 10-dollar notes, which he'd previously borrowed off Dean Jones and Tiffany Graham, and the stranger departed. As Chapman was about to bite the tablet in half, Tiffany came down the stairs.

She went over to him and asked, 'Hey, what are you doing?'

Chapman replied, 'Oh, it's a tablet. I'm just having half to see what it's like.' He then bit the tablet in half and Tiffany scooped up the other half and consumed it. Quite why she did that isn't clear, as she was known not to take illegal drugs. Perhaps she just wanted to see what the effects were like because later on she confided to Dean Jones, 'Ryan gave me a pill. This is the first time I've ever taken drugs.'

About half an hour later, she was talking to Jay Hornsey. 'I'm thirsty. I need water. Can you buy me a bottle? I had an eccky [ecstasy] and my mouth's dry.'

Hornsey dutifully went off to get her a bottle of water, and when he returned, she drank it down voraciously.

A little later on, the top section of Cooney's closed, so the group moved downstairs. Tiffany said she was still thirsty, and on that occasion, Dean Jones went off and got her another bottle of water. She drank most of it before carrying it outside, as Cooney's was closing for the night. After leaving the tavern at about 2.30 am, the group took a couple of taxis to Shaun Brooks's place at Mangerton. When they arrived at their destination, Tiffany stumbled getting out of the taxi, and Shaun Brooks and Jay Hornsey had to help to prevent her from falling over. Outside on the pavement, Tiffany started vomiting, soiling her clothing in the process.

'Shaun, please give me more water,' she pleaded.

She said she was very tired, so her friends put her to bed, where she fell asleep and began to snore loudly. In the meantime, Ryan Chapman appeared to be high and started to annoy the others with his continual pestering. Tiffany then woke up and joined her friends in the lounge, where she sat next to Dean Jones, putting her arms around him and saying, 'Don't let me go. I feel funny.' Then she vomited and collapsed.

Her shocked friends picked her up and carried her outside so she could get some fresh air, and when she seemed to be breathing normally, they took her back into the house and put her back in bed, where she slept and snored loudly for quite some time. But the worst was yet to come.

At about 4.20 am, Dean Jones went to check on her, but when he entered the room, he was greeted by blood and vomit coming out of her nose and mouth.

'Get an ambulance, there's something very wrong with Tiff,' he yelled.

At that stage, she was starting to turn blue and the situation was becoming very serious. She needed oxygen and urgent medical attention. Prior to the arrival of ambulance officers, Jones made some heroic attempts to save her, including mouth-to-mouth respiration and CPR. Unfortunately, it was a race against time because her lungs were filling up with fluid.

The ambulance arrived at 4.30 am and the paramedics intubated her at the scene. However, she didn't respond and was found to be asystolic (no electrical activity in the heart). The paramedics carried out their cardiac arrest procedures and she was shocked three times.

While they were working, Ryan Chapman turned to Dean Jones and Jay Hornsey and said, 'I suppose you're blaming me for this,' to which Dean Jones replied, 'Aw, piss off.'

Getting no response from their administrations, the paramedics drove Tiffany to Wollongong Hospital, arriving at 5.20 am. An intravenous drip was inserted into her arm and adrenaline administered in an effort to get her heart beating, even though the pupils of her eyes were fixed and dilated. CPR was also continued in the faint hope of recovery, but sadly, she was declared dead at 5.30 am by Dr Fraser.

A blood sample taken at the autopsy was found to contain MDMA 1.0 milligrams per litre, lignocaine 3.3 milligrams per litre and alcohol 0.024 grams per decilitre (100 millilitres) of blood. The lignocaine was most likely administered by medical personnel to counter the cardiotoxic effects, such as cardiac arrhythmia brought about by the MDMA, while the small amount of alcohol would have been a residual level left over from the previous evening's drinks. However, the level of MDMA in her blood was particularly high, well within the toxic range, and certainly lethal for a novice user.

Adverse reactions to MDMA include an increased heart rate, hypertension (raised blood pressure) progressing to hypotension (low blood pressure), nausea and vomiting, blurred vision, palpitations, hyperthermia, hyponatremia and renal failure.

One of the side effects of MDMA can be the impaired ability of the body to handle water, leading to hyponatraemia (essentially low sodium or salt level), which in turn gives rise to cerebral oedema, resulting in brain swelling and death. Unfortunately, that's what happened to Tiffany. Her brain was quite swollen, with a number of cerebral haemorrhages apparent. That supported the vomiting she experienced, something which is consistent with raised intracranial pressure.

The inquest took place on 8 December 2003. It was obvious from the outset that Tiffany had been a popular, much-loved young woman.

Friends and family members openly wept during proceedings, and at one point, the coroner suggested that Tiffany's mother might like to leave the court to avoid further distress when the tape of the telephone call to the ambulance was going to be played. The tape contained the voices of two of her friends repeatedly telling ambulance officers, 'Tiff's not breathing man. Tiff's not breathing.' When ambulance officers asked about Tiffany's history, Jay Hornsey replied, 'She's had a bit to drink and she's had drugs as well.'

I explained at the inquest that the toxic level of ecstasy results in excessive water consumption, leading to a shift in brain fluids and brain swelling, which accounted for Tiffany needing to consume large amounts of water prior to her death. I estimated that she would have had to have ingested at least two to three tablets of a potency ranging between 100 and 150 milligrams of MDMA per tablet for a young woman weighing 72 kilograms to reach a blood level of 1 milligrams per litre (mg/L). That was at odds with the half a tablet which she had taken. (Levels as low as 0.11 mg/L of ecstasy have caused fatalities in susceptible individuals, but Tiffany's MDMA level was much higher.)

So, the question to be asked was where did the additional ecstasy come from? One possibility was drink spiking, a thought that must have crossed the mind of Sergeant Kristy Spiers, an officer assisting the coroner, who asked me if I'd ever come across 'ecstasy in drink spiking.

I referred to a case where friends of the victims had put ecstasy in drinks as a game because they wanted to see changes in mood and behaviour. When questioned further, I said that ecstasy was soluble and almost undetectable in drinks with a bitter edge, such as bitters, tonic, beers or lager, which could mask the flavour.

During the inquest, Tiffany's mother, Mrs Marnya Graham, told the court that it was common knowledge that young men in Wollongong would supply the girls with ecstasy, as it increased their libido, and she went on to say that although she knew some of her daughter's friends used drugs, she didn't believe they would want to harm her. Mrs Graham also told the coroner that she thought there were three possible ways her daughter could have come to have taken ecstasy, namely a friend had given it to her, she'd asked for it, or she'd licked it off a friend's fingers. However, she then said, 'She wouldn't have taken it, she wouldn't have asked for it, and she wouldn't have licked it off his (a friend's) fingers.'

It was a view supported by Tiffany's brother, Ben Graham, who told the inquest that his sister had often criticised him for smoking and so he couldn't accept that she would have asked for a tablet of ecstasy. He said he was 100 per cent positive that there was no chance she would have taken the tablet.

It became quite evident from her friends and other witnesses that Tiffany had been opposed to drugs and had never had more than one or two drinks. The latter observation was supported by the fact that her blood alcohol level was just 0.024 grams per decilitre.

I subsequently concluded that I was of the opinion that Ms Graham ingested a lethal quantity of 3, 4-Methylenedioxymethamphetamine (MDMA), with death resulting from excessive water consumption leading to hyponatraemia (low blood saline levels) and cerebral oedema (excessive water on the brain). MDMA not only makes people thirsty and drink excessively, it also makes them retain water, greatly increasing risks all round.

Tiffany's was a particularly sad case. She'd gone to a tavern to enjoy an evening with friends, only to wind up dead from a drug overdose, an event made all the more poignant because she'd been opposed to drugs. Unfortunately, we'll never know whether her death might have been preventable after she'd ingested the ecstasy, but we do know that her death would have been prevented had she not ingested the drug in the first place.

And the big question still remains: who gave her the final lethal dose?

If you have any information that may assist the Wollongong investigators, please call Crime Stoppers on 1800 333 000.

Dianne Elizabeth Brimble.

12.

Death on the High Seas:
The Dianne Brimble Case

'Life isn't fair.
It's just fairer than death,
that's all.'
William Goldman

The morning of 23 September 2002 was humid, cool and cloudy, with the thermometer hovering at around 18 degrees Centigrade. At midday, give or take a few minutes, a new load of passengers arrived at Sydney's Darling Harbour Wharf 8 to board the cruise ship, the *Pacific Sky*, for a cruise around the Pacific. Among them was Dianne Brimble, who was very excited, because after saving for two years, the day had finally arrived for her holiday of a lifetime.

Dianne, a divorced suburban mother of three children worked full-time as a furniture store saleswoman in Brisbane, Queensland. She was accompanied by her 12-year-old daughter, Tahlia Michell, her older sister, and regular traveller, Alma Wood, and her daughter, Kari-Anne, also 12 years old. All four of them were going to share a cabin. The first port of call for the tourists was to be Noumea, scheduled for Thursday 26 September. They couldn't wait.

Unbeknown to them, a number of male passengers, later to be known as the 'eight persons of interest' also boarded the ship. They were Mark Wilhelm, Matthew Slade, Dragan Losic, Petar 'Pete' Pantic, Sakaleros 'Charlie' Kambouris, Letterio 'Leo' Silvestri, Luigi Vitale and Ryan Kuchel, and together they were to have a major impact on Dianne and her holiday. As fate would have it, the eight men were staying in two cabins (D182 and D178, across from each other) on the same corridor as Dianne and her party (D188).

They were all from Adelaide, all had somewhat 'colourful' backgrounds and all displayed antisocial behaviour from the moment the ship left port. At the time, Dragan Losic, a 41-year-old father of three, had 27 convictions and two jail sentences under his belt, one of three and a half years for drug offences. His many convictions included one for carrying an offensive weapon when he was 20, and breaking and entering. He'd also beaten a rape charge at the age of 18. In 2001, he'd been placed on a good behaviour bond after pleading guilty to being in possession of 1840 cannabis plants. Sakaleros Kambouris had written a character reference for the trial, in which he described Losic as a 'devoted father and family man who was trustworthy, reputable and a man of honour'.

Luigi Vitale had convictions for producing drugs, assault and possessing an unlicensed firearm. Mark Wilhelm had allegedly admitted to having and taking the drug 'fantasy', a street name for the chemical, gamma-hydroxybutyrate (GHB).

Letterio, or Leo (as he preferred to be called) Silvestri was no stranger to the courts either. He'd been charged with amphetamine possession on 12 September 2001 and had been convicted on a number of counts of fraud. On 2 February 2000, he'd pleaded guilty to 16 counts of falsely obtaining social security benefits and had subsequently been given a four-month suspended sentence.

Quite an unsavoury lot, and they were now onboard, primed and ready to offer illegal substances to young female passengers as they got ready for a 'fun-packed' night of drugs and debauchery.

The first evening on board began innocently enough. Dianne was enjoying herself immensely, drinking, dancing and socialising in the Legends Sports Bar with a number of adults, including her sister, Alma, and Gamu Chard, the son of some friends who were also travelling. With a few rum and cokes down her neck, she was in a festive mood, but as a lady who loved dancing, she found the music too light to really 'get down' and had to wait until 11 pm when the Starlight Disco opened with more exciting music. Around 9 pm, Alma left the dance floor to check on the children, Tahlia and Kari-Anne, and about an hour later, Dianne also went back to their cabin to kiss her daughter goodnight and freshen up, saying to Nancy Chard, one of the group, 'See you later.'

Dianne and Gamu headed for the Starlight Disco when it opened, getting straight onto the dance floor, leaving their drinks on their table. Taking a break from time to time, they'd return to sit down, rest and order refills.

The alcohol clearly emboldened Dianne, as she approached several men for a dance, one of whom she'd met earlier at the bar, purchasing drinks. His name was Dragan Losic. He was a guy who stood out; a big fellow, about 193 centimetres tall (6 feet 4 inches), broad-shouldered and with a distinctive goatee beard. It was 1.51 am.

'How's your holiday going?' he asked.

'Fine,' Dianne replied, and they carried on chatting for several minutes, exchanging all the usual small talk about where they were from, family and friends, et cetera.

After a while, Dragan said, 'Nice to meet you,' and took his drinks back to Petar Pantic, who was waiting at a nearby table.

By 2.30 am, the crowd had thinned out, leaving just a few of the more hardy passengers to carry on dancing and partying. Dianne and Gamu were sitting near some of the eight Adelaide men and started talking to them. Then, across the room, Dianne noticed a short man with thinning hair, Stephen Hart, who was working on the ship as a magician. Their eyes met and Dianne smiled at him. He walked over to her, had a brief chat and then asked her for a dance. Gamu was now sitting by himself, and after a little while, he decided to call it a night and head back to his cabin.

Meanwhile, Stephen Hart had taken a break from dancing with Dianne to drink his beer. On swallowing it, he found to his disgust that someone had dropped a cigarette into the glass. He excused himself to Dianne and left the disco to go back to his cabin.

At 3.30 am, half an hour before the official closing time for the disco, Dianne approached a group containing some of the Adelaide men and asked Dragan if she could join them. 'No worries,' he replied.

She then asked him if he'd like to dance with her. However, he declined, as he was talking to one of the ship's security guards, Olsen Va'aFusuaga (Mr V) about various matters. Dragan's close friend Petar then piped up, 'Do you mind, this is a private conversation.'

Dianne didn't take any offence and stayed with the group. Later, Ryan Kuchel joined them, and she asked *him* for a dance. Unfortunately, he'd been drinking most of the night and refused her offer, saying he was too tired. He subsequently left the group and went off to bed.

Dragan later suggested to Mark Wilhelm, who was also with the group, that he should take Dianne for a dance, which he did. After their dance, the pair rejoined the group, and following a few playful advances towards Dragan, which met with Petar's obvious disapproval, Dianne turned her attentions back to Mark.

At about 4.20 am, they all decided it was time to leave and go back to their cabins. The three men, Dragan, Petar and Mark, walked out of the disco with Dianne, but the group split up with Dragan and Petar going one way and Dianne and Mark another. Down on the deck below, an intoxicated and staggering Dianne pulled Mark into the female toilets to give him oral sex, behaviour that was most unlike her, but Mark, who was aroused from the stimulation she gave him, felt uncomfortable about what she was doing, so he stopped her and took her back to his cabin, D182.

When they got there, it was dark and quiet, and the other three occupants seemed to be asleep, so they climbed onto Mark's top bunk and had consensual vaginal sex, with Mark ejaculating early as a consequence of the alcohol he'd consumed and possibly drugs in his system. Dianne was very unhappy with his performance, telling him he was a dud root and that it was the worst sex she'd had in a long time.

It then became apparent that not all the other occupants of the room were asleep, as Leo Silvestri offered Mark a Viagra tablet. Dianne climbed down from Mark's bunk and began giving oral sex to Leo, who was on the lower left bunk in the cabin. Mark decided to leave them to it, as the Viagra didn't appear to be working, and he left the cabin, still naked, but for some unknown reason, he collected a life jacket on the way.

He went into cabin D156, occupied by Natasha McCann, Lisa Davis, Kelly Davis (Lisa's sister) and Tanya Power, where Dragan Losic, Petar Pantic and Ryan Kuchel were chatting to the young women. One of the men left the cabin and came back a few minutes later, holding a glass bottle with a clear liquid that had a pink tinge to it. He told the young women it was fantasy. In the meantime, Mark kept going in and out of the room. He eventually sobered up a little and returned to his own cabin, where he put on some boxer shorts. On returning once more, he and the other men each took a capful of the liquid. Ryan Kuchel passed out almost immediately (most likely because of the combination of the fantasy and the alcohol that was already in his system). The bottle was then offered to the young women, who wisely turned down the chance to imbibe.

Meanwhile, Charlie Kambouris had awoken from his slumber in D178 and gone across the corridor to D182, looking for Dragan and Petar. There, he saw not only Dianne lying on the floor, but also that she had defecated herself. He then went to D156 and told them what he'd seen and said that Mark had to clean her up, as the whole cabin smelt.

By that time, sunlight was creeping through the portholes of the cabins. Dawn had broken.

Mark went back to his cabin, where he saw a naked Dianne lying on top of a blanket, on the floor, with faeces on her buttocks. He wiped her backside and felt for a pulse, finding only a faint one. He woke Leo, and with his assistance, they carried Dianne into the shower, where they tried to wake her. Unfortunately, the cold water didn't do the trick and mucilage had started coming out of her mouth. It didn't look good. They carried her back to the bedroom and laid her on the floor between the bunks. With Leo's assistance, Mark dressed her after attempting expired air resuscitation. A further problem then presented itself in that a number of people had started moving along the corridors, most likely to get breakfast. The situation was looking desperate.

Lisa Davis rang cabin D182 at 8.45 am and spoke to Mark, who replied that there was something going down and that he couldn't talk. Shortly afterwards, he called for medical assistance and a Code Alpha (medical emergency) call went out over the PA system for cabin D182. The medical staff arrived promptly, led by a nurse, Donna Winter, who saw Dianne's cyanosed (blue colour) body, which was unresponsive, not breathing and with no pulse. Her jeans were wet around the groin area, and it was thought that she was incontinent of urine, but on further examination, the wetness was found to be due to the shower she'd been given by Mark and Leo earlier. The rest of the medical team arrived and ushered Mark out of the cabin so they could commence attempts to resuscitate Dianne.

Unfortunately, they were unsuccessful, and she was pronounced dead at 9.03 am on 24 September; the official cause of death being recorded as 'cardiac arrest due to unknown causes'. However, the post-mortem and toxicology reports that would determine the real cause of death were yet to be done.

The death was reported to Marine Area Command and they, in consultation with police commanders, crime agencies and various other bodies, including legal services and P&O Cruises, began an immediate enquiry. Senior Constable Erdinc 'Dinch' Ozen of the Marine Area Command investigative group contacted Mike Drake, the operations manager of the South Pacific at P&O to order cabin D182 and Dianne Brimble's cabin, D188, to be sealed off and a crime scene guard placed outside.

Marine Area Command was used to dealing with deaths aboard cruise ships and other marine vessels, but this one proved to be quite different, as following a conference with crime agencies, a number of cross-territorial issues were revealed.

The cruise ship was about 90 nautical miles off the coast of New South Wales, with the next scheduled port of call being Noumea, New Caledonia, where it would arrive on 26 September, two days later. It was agreed that two investigators, a crime scene officer and a fingerprint officer would be flown to Noumea to meet the ship and begin their investigations. Forensic officers, including a pathologist, would only carry out the post-mortem on the body when it was returned to Sydney.

On 25 September, Acting Sergeant Victor Rulewski and Senior Constable Erdinc Ozen flew to Noumea to await the arrival of the cruise ship. The crime scene and fingerprint officers were due in the following day.

At 7.30 am on Thursday 26 September, Acting Sergeant Victor Rulewski and Senior Constable Erdinc Ozen met the *Pacific Sky* at the dock, making contact with Captain le-Metre and the chief officers of New Caledonian Quarantine and Federal Police, together with the ship's captain, staff captain, chief of security and other staff members, including the ship's senior doctor, Dr Damien McAliskey, who considered Dianne's death suspicious because a tablet had been found near her body, suggesting she may have died from a drug overdose.

The detectives then met Alma Wood, Dianne's sister, who, after brief introductions, was taken to the medical centre of the ship, where she formally identified the deceased. Dianne's body was then released and sent back to Sydney, where it would undergo a post-mortem to determine her cause of death.

The police officers then took a statement from Alma in order to establish Dianne's movements up to and including 24 September. She said her sister had been in good spirits and had been a heavy social drinker, but hadn't been known to take drugs. She hadn't been depressed or had any major medical problems other than some respiratory problems, which included chest infections, sinus and asthma. Alma was then allowed to collect her passport and possessions from the cabin so she could fly back to Australia with the children.

Next to be interviewed were the 'eight persons of interest', beginning with Mark Wilhelm, via a portable ERISP (Electronically Recorded Interview of a Suspected Person). He gave two security incident reports, in which he didn't admit to drug usage, although, on the second, he stated that he'd taken four ecstasy tablets on board, two of which he'd taken on the evening of 23 September, throwing the other two overboard after the incident. He emphatically denied supplying anyone with any drug.

Next up was Letterio 'Leo' Silvestri, who said he didn't want to be formally interviewed in relation to the matter, but eventually agreed to make a statement. He said he'd been intoxicated on the evening of 23 September and had taken three sleeping tablets, so he couldn't remember anything. However, he did recall seeing, in his words, 'an ugly fat black bitch' on his bunk, whom he'd pushed off, onto the floor of the cabin. He denied supplying drugs to anyone.

Matthew Slade said he'd gone to sleep early that evening, as he'd had a few drinks and taken a sleeping tablet given to him by Leo Silvestri. When he'd woken up early the following morning, wanting to have a cigarette, he'd got out of bed and seen Mark Wilhelm and Leo Silvestri near the doorway of the bathroom. He said their voices had sounded panicky.

Ryan Kuchel said he'd seen Mark Wilhelm having sex with Dianne Brimble, but had left shortly afterwards to speak to some people in the corridor. He'd later gone to cabin D156 (which he misidentified as D146), where he'd fallen asleep, waking up later that morning. It's probable he'd passed out from a combination of alcohol and a capful of fantasy (GHB).

In the meantime, Senior Sergeant Newell from the fingerprint examination unit and Sergeant Cairnduff from the crime scene unit began their examination of cabin D182, but as the occupants had been allowed to enter cabins D182 and D178 and take their belongings, the crime scene had been severely compromised.

After Acting Sergeant Victor Rulewski and Senior Constable Erdinc Ozen concluded their interviews for the day, they reported back to their Sydney office before deciding to explore the ship and mingle with the passengers, thinking that people might be more willing to open up and talk to them in a more informal environment. Just after 8 pm, they met up with the four young women, Lisa Davis, her sister Kellie, and their two friends, Tanya and Natasha, who were socialising in the Piano Lounge. Since Dianne's death they'd become nervous and, as they said later, they were very frightened after seeing the two men standing near the dance floor, 'glaring' at them.

Detective Senior Constable Ozen approached them. 'Which of you ladies would like to dance with me?'

Lisa volunteered, and during the waltz said, 'I think you need to speak with us girls.'

'Why? Ozen asked. 'Which cabin are you in?'

'D156.'

When Lisa told him that various men had been going in and out of their cabin on the fateful morning, one naked save for a life jacket, Ozen agreed with her opening statement.

On 27 September, the remainder of the 'eight persons of interest', namely Dragan Losic, Luigi Vitale, Petar Pantic and Sakaleros 'Charlie' Kambouris were scheduled to be interviewed, but they refused without the presence of their lawyer and wouldn't even give a brief version of events.

However, the four young women from D156 were more forthcoming. They described the goings on during the night, including the activities of the men that came to their cabin. Of particular interest was the water bottle that contained a liquid with a pink tinge to it. The young women said they'd refused it when offered, and the men had left it in their cabin.

A search was begun, but the liquid wasn't to be found, although some exhibits were collected from the other cabins in question, including D182, and forwarded on to the appropriate laboratories for examination in the hope some tangible evidence might be gleaned from them.

While the crime scene had been compromised, as luck would have it, a valuable piece of evidence had inadvertently been saved. On the evening of 24 September, two days prior to the arrival of the Sydney detectives, a young boy of primary school age had been wandering in the lobby where the ship's purser's desk was located. He'd come across a rectangular purple plastic object and, not realising what it was, had handed it in to Michael Boulton, a junior purser. Thinking nothing more of it, Boulton had entered the object into a lost property register and placed it into a box in the lost property safe. The following morning, he'd been working with another junior assistant purser, Michael Edgeworth, who'd recognised the object as a 64 MB Sony memory stick from a digital camera. Prior to that, the P&O staff had been briefed about the circumstances surrounding Dianne Brimble's death and advised to be vigilant about the men from Adelaide, so Edgeworth had deleted the entry from the register and inserted the memory stick into his camera to find out what was on it. He saw lots of photographs of people socialising on the ship, but, more importantly, he recognised some of the members of the group of eight from Adelaide. Realising the information could be vital for those investigating Dianne's death, he'd handed the stick to a senior officer, Russell Walters, who gave it to the police several days later. In turn, they put it into an exhibit bag, for later examination by experts in Sydney.

In the meantime, Dragan Losic and Charlie Kambouris called around to the purser's desk to enquire about the missing memory stick, but there was no record of it in the register and it couldn't be found in the safe.

Back in Sydney, a police computer expert examined the 64 MB memory stick and found 41 JPEG files on it. They initially consisted of regular family snaps, but, on probing further, he found records of 156 deleted image files and 26 deleted video files. He was able to restore many of the deleted image files, including 30 files from 23 and 24 September, which were to provide information as to what had happened on the night in question. The video files, however, had been overwritten and could not be accessed.

Among the first batch of retrieved photos was one recorded at 12.18 pm on 23 September, which showed a group shot of the eight men from Adelaide outside the Sydney cruise ship terminal 8. However, the remaining 22 image files (depicting sexual acts and several shots of Dianne's prone body with faeces on her buttocks, with several disturbing close-ups) were recorded between 4.50 am and 6.32 am on Tuesday 24 September, providing a graphic insight into the night of drugs and depravities which had led up to the tragedy. Consequently, they were of great help to the police investigation.

Nevertheless, it took about four years of interviews and investigations, coupled with numerous problems such as health issues with Senior Constable Erdinc Ozen, before a formal inquest into Dianne Brimble's death on the *Pacific Sky* cruise ship was finally implemented.

Her body arrived at the Glebe Department of Forensic Medicine on the morning of 27 September 2002. The ship's doctor, Dr Damian McAliskey, stated on his certificate that her cause of death was 'cardiac arrest due to an unknown cause', a standard statement to describe an unknown cause of death. He further added, 'The death was not due [to] a communicable or contagious disease, nor HIV related.'

The post-mortem was carried out by Dr Johan Duflou, at 10 am on 28 September. A number of minor injuries were observed on Dianne's body. There was suffusion (a widespread reddening) of her face, but no evidence of neck compression or other cause of obstruction of the airway. However, there was fluid accumulation in her lungs and all of her organs were reportedly congested. Such symptoms are typical of an over dosage of a central nervous system (CNS) depressant or a combination of CNS depressants.

That conclusion was borne out by the subsequent toxicology report, which revealed that a blood sample taken at post-mortem was found to contain gamma-hydroxybutyrate (GHB) 210 milligrams per litre and alcohol 0.127 grams per 100 millilitres of blood. Dianne's stomach contents also contained GHB 6300 milligrams per litre and liver fluid GHB 120 milligrams per litre. That clearly indicated an overdose of GHB, which had been exacerbated by the alcohol already in her system from an evening of drinking.

The inquest finally got underway on Monday 9 March 2006. It was conducted by the Senior Deputy State Coroner Jacqueline Milledge, a former police prosecutor who had been working at the coroner's court for seven years and had seen her share of tragedies. Her assisting council was Mr Ron Hoenig, a criminal barrister who had previously carried out much of his work in the Supreme Court. He began his opening address by stating, 'Dianne Brimble was killed by some person or persons, by someone slipping her a lethal dose of a date-rape drug without her knowledge for the sole purpose of their own sexual gratification and the sexual assault and abuse of Mrs Brimble.'

He then outlined what the police knew about what had occurred on the *Pacific Sky* and the evidence provided by witnesses.

He concluded with, 'The evidence will clearly show that Mrs Brimble was killed. The evidence will clearly show that Mrs Brimble, a dedicated mother of children, who took her youngest child on a cruise, no doubt using her life savings, was preyed upon by some people after having had administered to her a substance that broke her will or interfered with any ability for her to say 'yes' or 'no'. As a result she was subject to terrible degradation which no human being, let alone a female, should be subjected to. And the way in which somebody who themselves is a prude about their own body and covers themselves up to be found in the undignified way in which she was found is nothing short of absolutely reprehensible.'

After that opening address, further evidence was provided by family members and David Mitchell, Dianne's long-term partner and Tahlia's father, as to Dianne's modest, prudish nature.

Naturally, all of Australia's major newspapers ran the story the following day, and for the next three years, the story and people involved were rarely out of the news media.

I eventually became caught up in the inquest after issuing a statement regarding the amount of gamma hydroxybutyrate (GHB) and alcohol detected in Dianne's body at the post-mortem. In my report I stated in part, after providing some background to the drug, the following:

Ms Brimble's blood level was 210 milligrams per litre (along with alcohol at 0.127 grams per decilitre). Single doses of GHB

(25 mg/kg) produce peak serum levels of 24–102 milligrams per litre. Doses of 50 mg/kg produce peak levels of 48–124 milligrams per litre. Given Ms Brimble's weight of 86 kg then, it would appear she would have ingested over 7 grams (and possibly as high as ~18 grams) of GHB. Therefore, it would appear Ms Brimble either received more than one dose of GHB or that she received a rather large dose (probably, in her drink/s) prior to the disco closing, with the possibility of a further dose thereafter. This is supported by the elevated blood level of GHB and the fact that there was still some GHB present in her stomach contents.

On Thursday 16 November 2006, I attended Glebe Coroner's Court and was cross-examined regarding the effects of GHB. I described the drug, also known as fantasy and liquid ecstasy, as a 'colourless to pale pink, odourless, slightly salty tasting liquid freely soluble in water and thereby, can be readily added undetected to drinks at parties and dances. It is a drug which is often used in cases of date rape.'

I was certain Dianne Brimble had had more than one dose and that she could have been topped up throughout the evening and early morning, an observation supported by her behaviour when she'd left the disco in the early morning, and I suggested that the first dose could have been taken in the ship's nightclub between three and four o'clock in the morning.

Mr Ron Hoenig, the assisting counsel, asked me what Dianne Brimble's chances of surviving such a dose had been. I had no choice but to answer, 'I'm sorry to say, virtually none.'

That was due to the fact that she'd had *both* alcohol and GHB in her blood, and *both* at elevated levels. Furthermore, GHB had been present in her stomach contents, most likely from a more recent ingestion, and had provided a source of further absorption into her blood, thus sealing her fate.

I was called back to the inquest on 27 November 2006 and subjected to a rigorous cross-examination by Mr John Sheahan, senior counsel, and P&O's senior barrister because my earlier testimony apparently had potential implications for P&O's liability, and the culpability of the 'eight persons of interest'.

Under cross-examination, I admitted my calculations had just been estimates and ballpark figures and the problem was that since then, a great deal of credence had been placed on them. For example, the figures I'd previously given regarding the range of how much GHB Dianne would have appeared to have ingested was based on GHB consumption and subsequent blood levels detected in the literature and from casework.

GHB exhibits nonlinear kinetics, such that in higher doses, it causes increases in absorption and elimination half-lives (the time it takes for a drug to drop to half its previous level) and the time to peak the blood concentration after consuming the drug orally (the usual mode of ingestion). In other words, it's not possible to carry out a back calculation like those done for alcohol intoxication.

I had merely sought to show that it had been more than likely that Dianne had received more than one dose of GHB (allegedly a capful from a water bottle). Given an average cap on a standard water bottle is about 8 millilitres and GHB solution about 50 per cent (the alleged solution had a pink tinge), the dose provided by just one capful would have been about 4 grams and two capfuls about 8 grams, which is well within the ballpark figure. However, street drugs are often of questionable purity.

Another expert, Dr David Caldicott, a specialist commissioned by Mark Wilhelm, told the inquest that it was possible Dianne had taken more than one dose of GHB, but that there was no way of knowing for sure. Effectively, agreeing with my conclusions.

Meanwhile, the police had been busy conducting a number of further investigations, including the recording of phone calls of the 'eight persons of interest'. They resulted in what became known as the 'The Brimble Tapes', providing valuable information to the inquest.

After 66 hearing days and 17 months, the inquest finally reached a conclusion on the afternoon of 26 July 2007. NSW Deputy State Coroner Jacqueline Milledge ruled there was enough evidence to charge known persons over Dianne's death. She then spoke to the court, saying, 'I find that Dianne Elizabeth Brimble died on 24 September 2002 in cabin D182 of the P&O cruise ship *Pacific Sky*. I am satisfied that the evidence before me is capable of satisfying a jury beyond reasonable doubt that known persons have committed an indictable offence and that there is a reasonable prospect that a jury would convict the known persons of an indictable offence in relation to the cause of death of Mrs Brimble. I therefore terminate this inquest pursuant to section 19 of the Coroner's Act of 1980 and refer all the papers to the Director of Public Prosecutions (DPP).'

However, the brief, being the full complement of papers and materials from the coroner, didn't arrive at the office of the DPP until 21 January 2008, some six years after Dianne's lifeless body had been found in the cruise ship cabin.

The brief (a misnomer if ever there was) comprised 17 boxes of statements and exhibits, each needing sorting, analysis and comment. Given the department was under-resourced at the time, it was a lot to expect. However, after eight months of examining the evidence obtained from the coronial inquest, the DPP was able to recommend that three of the four men who had shared cabin D182, where Dianne's body had been, found should face charges. Mark Wilhelm should be charged with manslaughter and drug supply, for giving Dianne Brimble the drug GHB, while the other two men, Letterio 'Leo' Silvestri and Ryan Kuchel, should be charged with perverting the course of justice.

A statement was then issued from the DPP, announcing, 'Ex officio indictments for these charges have been filed in New South Wales with the district court regarding Silvestri and Kuchel and will be sought in the Supreme Court regarding Wilhelm.'

Mark Wilhelm's trial finally began in September 2009, seven years after Dianne Brimble's death. He appeared before Justice Roderick Howie at the Supreme Court in Taylor Square, Sydney. Justice Howie was an experienced appeal court judge who had presided over a number of high-profile cases down the years. The Crown prosecutor was Mark Hobart, senior counsel, and the defence barrister was George Thomas.

I was subsequently subpoenaed to appear on 14 September, but that was complicated by the presence of me and another three experts. The object of the exercise was to ascertain the extent of agreement and/or disagreement between the experts. A voir dire was held (a hearing by the judge in the absence of the jury) in which we had to give joint evidence regarding the matter. A voir dire with several experts is seldom used in criminal matters, and it caught me by surprise. Fortunately, we agreed on most of the important issues, the exception being when Dianne had died. I felt that she'd been in serious trouble, if not already dying, when she'd defecated herself, as GHB can cause incontinence.

That latter piece of information was of importance in relation to a duty of care by Mark Wilhelm and Leo Silvestri, but it soon became apparent that the prosecution did not have a strong case for Wilhelm to be found guilty of manslaughter by negligence, leaving the remaining charge of drug supply.

The jury's deliberations dragged on, as there was uncertainty as to whether the drug had significantly caused Dianne's death and whether Wilhelm could be held criminally responsible. In the end, the jurors were unable to agree, resulting in a hung jury and another trial.

After the trial, Mark Wilhelm's lawyers offered the DPP a deal: if they dropped the manslaughter charge, he would plead guilty to the drug supply charge.

In the meantime, both the prosecution and defence teams searched the Crimes Act, and found a seldom used charge of using a noxious substance to endanger life.

On 29 April 2010, days before Mark Wilhelm's second trial was to go ahead, the DPP agreed, and withdrew the manslaughter charge. Later, Mark Wilhelm pleaded guilty to supplying Dianne Brimble with GHB.

Supreme Court Justice Howie described the supply of GHB as 'a "social" or consensual one, with the evidence showing both Mr Wilhelm and Ms Brimble took the drug willingly, as adults, ahead of a sexual encounter. Therefore on the scale of supply, it must be on the absolute lowest range of such offences.' He then imposed a section 10, meaning no conviction was to be recorded.

He concluded, 'Finally it has come to an end and you can get on, hopefully, with the rest of your life the best as you are able.'

It was truly a sad end for an event that affected so many people, and all from a few drunken and drug-affected hours.

★

On 5 March 2013, Detective Senior Constable Erdinc Ozen, a Turkish-born Australian, passed away from a brain aneurism. He was just 41 years old. He'd previously retired from Marine Area Command on 29 September 2011, after completing 20 years of service. He'd been a fine, dedicated police officer, and his colleagues, including me, were greatly saddened by his passing. No doubt the stresses over the years since the death of Dianne Brimble and the subsequent inquest had taken their toll on his health.

The funeral service was held at Gelibolu Mosque in Auburn, Sydney on 8 March 2013, and unfortunately, this sad event was further marred by controversy when a Muslim cleric, told everyone that because it was a Muslim prayer service, women and non-Muslims were not welcome and had to leave the mosque area. Erdinc's brother, Tunc Ozen said, 'All of his friends were not Muslim, so they had to leave. It was a big shock. It upset a lot of people.'

But probably, the most hurtful and upsetting thing for Erdinc's family came when it was time to move his coffin because his closest friends were not allowed to take part in the proceedings.

Tunc Ozen further commented, 'These complete strangers were grabbing my brother's coffin, not his mates, as a result of what this bloke said. I've spent as much time thanking people for coming as I have apologising to them over what happened.'

The Islamic Friendship Association president, Keysar Trad, said, 'What was done does not run consistently with our traditions. Our religion teaches us to be compassionate towards people grieving.'

For right or wrong, what was done was done and can't be undone, but it won't change people's opinion of Detective Senior Constable Erdinc Ozen, and certainly not mine, and he will be remembered as a top cop who did his best, given the very difficult circumstances – and in the very first case of its kind in Australia.

Sarah Rawson.

13.

Mystery Cliff Top Fall:
The Sarah Rawson Case

'When ill luck begins,
it does not come in sprinkles,
but in showers.'
Mark Twain

Hargraves Lookout, a small, uneven rocky outcrop that provides magnificent views over the rural Megalong Valley is located at the southern end of Shipley Plateau, Blackheath, in the Blue Mountains of New South Wales. It was named in honour of William Henry Hargraves (1839–1925), the Deputy Registrar in Equity, who was once known as the father of Blackheath. However, in spite of its rugged beauty, it can be a very dangerous place for the unwary, as there was no barrier or fence between the ledge and a sheer cliff drop of several hundred metres. It's against that background that this sad story unfolds.

The 'picnic spot' on the small, uneven rocky outcrop at Hargraves Lookout.

At about 11.30 am on 11 March 2006, 23-year-old Shawn Mullen picked up Sarah Rawson, his new girlfriend of three weeks, from her home in Cambridge Park, Penrith, Sydney. She was an attractive young lady, two years Mullen's senior. They were just like any other regular dating couple, except for the fact that Sarah was wheelchair bound, having been involved in a horrific head-on car crash four months earlier, outside Ballina, NSW, which had resulted in 35 broken bones, including both arms and legs. Since then she'd relied on a wheelchair for mobility of more than a few metres, and only used crutches when absolutely necessary, as that method of movement proved to be more painful for her. But she wasn't one to brood about the unfairness of the world, and was determined to get on with her life, even booking a South Pacific cruise with her mother, who'd been helping her recover. Sarah was an easygoing, social, educator who worked with disabled and mentally ill people. She was very popular and enjoyed life, often being described as vibrant and beautiful.

It was their fourth date, and they spent a few hours sightseeing in Katoomba before deciding to have an early evening picnic at Hargraves Lookout. After buying a bottle of Omni Pink sparkling wine, a packet of crackers, some cheese and strawberries, Shawn placed Sarah into the passenger seat of his grey Holden Rodeo ute before loading her wheelchair into the back, along with the food and drink.

It was late afternoon when they arrived at their destination, and the area was deserted. An early evening mist was creeping up the Megalong Valley, the silence only being broken by the occasional sound from the bush birdlife. A peaceful, idyllic location. Shawn unloaded the vehicle and placed a picnic rug a few metres from the edge of the cliff. After helping Sarah onto the rug, the 'bubbly' was popped and the pair settled down to dine on the wine, cheese and crackers while enjoying the spectacular views over the valley below.

Around 5.45 pm, Sarah told Shawn that she needed to make a call of nature and asked him to look away, which he did. While his head was turned the other way, he heard a little scream, and when he turned back, Sarah was gone, having fallen 70 metres to her death over the cliff edge.

Mullen immediately rang 000, outlining to the operator what had happened. A police rescue team arrived, along with detectives and crime scene officers who examined the area, taking photographs of the scene, Shawn Mullen's grey Holden Rodeo and Sarah's body in its final resting place.

The rescue officers and forensic experts then abseiled down the cliff to examine Sarah's body, which was only winched up from the base of the cliff the following day because bad weather and poor visibility hampered its retrieval at the time. After gathering as much evidence as they could and taking a statement from Shawn Mullen, police went to inform Sarah's mother. Unfortunately, the timing couldn't have been worse. Margaret Rawson had arranged a party in her daughter's honour, and she and about 50 guests were waiting for Sarah to arrive. What should have been a joyous birthday celebration turned into a night of grief-stricken anguish.

After formal identification, Sarah's body was taken to the Department of Forensic Medicine, Westmead Hospital for a post-mortem, which was carried out by Dr Peter S. J. Ellis. He concluded that her death was due to the effect of multiple injuries, of which the most serious were severe head injury and damage to the neck and chest. These are consistent with a fall from a cliff. While blood and urine alcohol were elevated, there was nothing in the autopsy to suggest (or exclude) any altercation prior to the fall. It was quite a conservative report.

Sarah's funeral took place on a cold, drizzly Monday on 20 March 2006. The service was attended by family and friends, and her ashes were later scattered in Ballina, a town she loved and where she'd been planning to open a shop when she recovered from her many injuries. Shawn Mullen didn't attend the funeral nor did he see Sarah's family, despite having previously said he was devastated by her death.

An inquest was conducted by Mr Carl Milovanovich, the deputy state coroner, on 11 May 2009. At the centre of the enquiry was how mobile Sarah had been on the day of her death.

Shawn Mullen was the last person to have seen Sarah alive and he reiterated what he'd previously told police about his and Sarah's date up to the point when she disappeared over the cliff. He said how, despite her disability, he'd helped her over the barrier at the lookout, 3 metres from the edge of the cliff, before returning to his ute at close on 5.45 pm to collect her wheelchair, also claiming that she'd been keen to look around after being carried to the cliff edge. He told the inquest that he and Sarah had been intimate, after which she'd asked him to turn away while she urinated, even though there had been a toilet only a short distance away. He admitted he'd glanced back and seen that she'd been trying to pull up her jeans, but hadn't seen her fall. He'd then made the 000 call.

The coroner heard evidence that Sarah Rawson's worried friends had tried to warn her off Shawn Mullen a week before her death, calling him a 'psycho'. That seemed to be supported by Mullen's friends who said he was unusual, and also described him as obsessive and weird.

Detective Senior Constable John Fasano provided evidence that a former girlfriend of Shawn Mullen had dumped him because of his violent mood swings, saying, 'She stated that his depressive mood swings and raging temper stopped their relationship.'

The coroner was also told that Shawn Mullen had twice been admitted to Pialla psychiatric ward for treatment and that he had a history of mental illness, going back to 2001.

Detective Senior Constable Fasano also said he thought it strange that Sarah Rawson hadn't attempted to use the toilet that was about 25 metres away. In his view, he felt that it would be odd for a female to go to the toilet on the edge of a cliff without any toilet paper and in full view of any person who could have driven down the road at any time. However, he admitted he'd been unable to determine whether the toilet had been operational or open on the day Sarah had died.

Another police witness, Detective Senior Constable Jason Howe, told the court that Mullen heard a little scream, turned around and she was no longer there. In relation to the 000 call, he said that Mullen had asked if he would be charged with manslaughter before saying that he thought he'd be going to jail and that Sarah's body was in four pieces. Then Mullen had said he couldn't see her, and that he'd have to notify her parents, who would think it was his fault.

The detective then put before the inquest three possible scenarios: Firstly, he suggested that Ms Rawson fell from the cliff in the manner that Mullen described. Second, and to his mind equally likely, Mullen pushed her over the cliff. Finally, as Ms Rawson was being assisted back from the cliff edge by Mullen he accidentally dropped her, causing her to fall over the edge. That may have caused Mullen to construct a story to cover his perceived recklessness or negligence.

A number of other witnesses came forward and gave evidence in relation to the case, including myself. I was at the inquest to interpret the levels of drugs and alcohol detected in Sarah Rawson's blood sample, and so determine how much she would have been affected at the time of the tragedy. Shawn Mullen had previously said that Sarah Rawson had consumed two schooners of Tooheys New full-strength beer between 1 pm and 3 pm and more than half of the 750 ml bottle of Omni Pink (11.5% alcohol) sparkling wine just prior to her death. Sarah had been used to drinking alcohol and had been taking the drug sertraline for four weeks. The analyst's reports, carried out by the Division of Analytical Laboratories in Lidcombe in Sydney, showed the following levels of the drug and alcohol in the blood sample taken at post-mortem: sertraline 0.2 milligrams per litre and alcohol 0.150 grams per decilitre (100 millilitres) of blood. Her urine sample was found to have present alcohol 0.208 grams per decilitre (100 millilitres) of urine. I calculated Sarah's likely blood alcohol level at the time of her death to have been 0.150 grams per decilitre, and found to my surprise that the drinking history the inquest had been provided with was quite accurate. (Quite often, they're either understated or overstated, depending upon the circumstances!)

I told the inquest that level of sertraline or Zoloft was not an issue, as Sarah had been taking the drug for about four weeks to treat anxiety and depression and it was within the therapeutic level needed for treatment of that condition. However, the level of alcohol in her blood would have affected her faculties and, given her proximity to the cliff edge, impaired her ability to react effectively in an emergency situation. Essentially, she would have been under the influence of alcohol and in a very vulnerable situation which could have led to the fatal outcome.

After some consideration, Mr Milovanovich found that Sarah Rawson had died from multiple injuries following an accidental fall from a cliff edge at Hargraves Lookout, near Blackheath, on 11 March 2006. He commented, after having examined all the evidence, it was the view of the court that Sarah's death was a tragic accident. He also recommended that Blue Mountains City Council examine the site where Sarah had fallen to her death and consider more fencing and better signage because of its proximity to a car park. He was also concerned that the rock ledge was adjacent to a car park and young children could easily run out of vehicles or wander into this area and not be aware of the potential danger. Similarly, adults may not be aware of the sudden cliff drop and the uneven surface.

Since the coroner's recommendation to Blue Mountains City Council, only a token barrier fence has been erected adjacent to the car park, and a sign on a pole, depicting a stick figure in danger, has been placed at the tragic site in lieu of a safety fence.

While it is a beautiful scene over the Megalong Valley, I personally believe a barrier fence should be installed to protect the foolhardy and to respect the death of a beautiful young woman. Perhaps a plaque should be erected in her memory, which may also provide a warning to other visitors to the site.

Murder victim: Pia Navida.

14.
Sex, Drugs and a Body in the Bush:
The Pia Navida Case

'Man is the cruelest animal.'

Friedrich Nietzsche

Pia Kate Navida was an attractive Filipino teenager who migrated to Australia from the Philippines in the early 1980s as a very young bride of an Australian national. Treasured by her family, she was a young woman full of hope and promise. Physically, she was a real stunner with a shapely body, beautiful golden skin, almond-shaped eyes and lovely dark hair. But underneath all that outward beauty lurked a fiery temper. Eventually, her somewhat laid-back husband couldn't take her angry outbursts anymore and they divorced, leaving Pia in a terrible financial situation. To make ends meet, she resorted to prostitution and adopted a nomadic lifestyle, which brought her into contact with a number of undesirables and led her to embrace the drug scene, in particular, the stimulant methylamphetamine (also known as speed).

Pia Navida's favourite haunts were in the area around Sydney's Central railway station, where she solicited for sex in bars, as well as at Greasey's Cafe in Elizabeth Street, a short walk away. She had several boyfriends, but treated them more as a convenience than as partners in a satisfying mutual relationship. Rather than pleasing her lovers, it was more a case of them pleasing her. Perhaps her work as a prostitute made her feel it was her turn for some enjoyment.

At 1 pm, on Friday 31 January 1992, she was at the Central Station bar, having drinks with friends, when she met up with a potential customer who offered her a lift. She accepted, and that was the last time she was seen alive.

The following day, around 12 o'clock, some bushwalkers were trekking by Bundeena, a quaint village surrounded by the Royal National Park on the outskirts of southern Sydney, about 29 kilometres from Sydney's central business district, when they came across some clothing scattered across the bush track. An orange-coloured face washer hung on a branch nearby.

Puzzling over where the clothing might have come from, the walkers soon stumbled upon the battered naked body of Pia Navida. It was on a service track known as Marley's Beach Trail. She was lying on her back and it looked like she'd been bludgeoned to death. A large, 14-kilogram bloodstained sandstone rock, the probable murder weapon, lay nearby. It was a shocking discovery.

The police were promptly called, the area sealed off, and the witnesses interviewed. It was determined she'd been raped and then bludgeoned to death with the large sandstone rock, which had crushed her face, making her barely recognisable. Her body had then been dragged a short distance and dumped where it was found.

After her body had been taken to the Glebe morgue in Sydney, the police investigation began in earnest. Strike Force Ever, comprising detectives from the state crime command's unsolved homicide team, was established to investigate the circumstances surrounding her death.

Investigating police were certain that more than one culprit had been involved, and a number of suspects, including Wayne Taylor, a man with whom she'd had a somewhat volatile, and at times violent, relationship were investigated and cleared. Sadly, the investigation then appeared to have reached a dead end.

A number of samples were taken from Pia's body at the post-mortem for toxicological examination. Her blood sample was found to have present methamphetamine 1.0 milligrams per litre and pseudoephedrine 0.15 milligrams per litre, while a liver sample was found to contain 0.2 milligrams per kilogram of methylamphetamine, her stomach sample 0.23 milligrams per litre of methylamphetamine and 0.07 milligrams of pseudoephedrine, and her urine sample 13 milligrams per litre of methylamphetamine and pseudoephedrine 7.3 milligrams per litre, along with cannabinoids (cannabis products).

This toxicology profile provided a number of pieces of evidence that I later provided to the Supreme Court at Taylor Square, Darlinghurst.

Firstly, her blood level for methylamphetamine ('meth') showed she'd clearly been a seasoned meth user. The therapeutic range (the 'feel good' level) for this drug is 0.01 to 0.05 milligrams per litre. Pia's blood level was well outside this range. The pseudoephedrine could have come from a number of sources, an impurity in the original methylamphetamine source or from a flu medication. However, methylamphetamine is readily synthesised from pseudoephedrine.

Secondly, the presence of the drug in her stomach contents indicated that she had taken the drug orally, and because some of it was still there (it hadn't all been absorbed into her blood stream), it indicated recent usage. Methylamphetamine can be taken orally (by mouth), intra nasally (snorting the powder), injected or by smoking. Users may become dependent upon the drug and use it with increasing frequency and in larger doses to get the same desired effect.

Additional forensic samples, including swabs and fingernail clippings were also taken from Pia's body at the post-mortem. Those specimens were stored in a refrigerator and later proved to be very useful for further future (cold case) investigations into the murder.

In 1994, an inquest into Pia's death was held, returning an open finding as to who took her life under such brutal circumstances. And there the matter lay until much needed advances in DNA technology took place.

But fortunately, science never sleeps, and 12 years later, an identifiable DNA profile was extracted from the semen swabs taken from both the interior and exterior of Pia Navida's body. The profiles were uploaded into the now established national DNA database, which had begun to yield some very worthwhile results for a number of cold cases, and matches were made with a man known as Steven Isaac Matthews and another two males. Unfortunately, the evidence didn't appear to be sufficient to convict the suspects, but with further testing, in 2011, it was found that semen swab samples taken from Pia's body were consistent with the DNA profiles of two males, Rodney James Paterson and Steven Isaac Matthews.

It appeared that both Steven Matthews and Rodney Paterson had had sex with Pia Navida prior to her death, but police still had to ascertain who had done the final foul deed. The crime scene had seemed to indicate more than one participant was involved, so the police swung into action and arrested both men.

Rodney Paterson was arrested in Bathurst, and first appeared at Bathurst Local Court. He didn't apply for bail, which had been formally refused anyway, and reappeared at the Central Local Court in Sydney. In the meantime, police successfully sought the extradition of Steven Matthews, who was arrested near Melbourne. He was then transported across the border to Albury, where he was formally charged at Albury Local Court with murder and sexual assault. As expected, bail was refused. The matter then went before the Supreme Court in Taylor Square, Darlinghurst before Justice Geoffrey Bellew on 3 February 2014. That was just over 22 years after Pia Navida's violent sexual assault and murder.

Matthews pleaded guilty to both rape and murder. He even said that he'd taken a girlfriend for picnics to Bundeena, where Pia Navida's body had been found, and told her he'd killed a person in the bush area before showing her how he'd carried it out. He also told the court that he, too, had been a victim of a major assault, in 2005, which had left him with a serious brain injury and little memory of his earlier life.

Paterson maintained his innocence regarding both charges. He initially denied knowing Pia Navida, although he did admit he may have met her at the bar she used to frequent near the Central railway station. However, he later changed his story, stating that he had, in fact, had consensual sex with her before her death.

The Crown pointed out that Paterson's DNA had been found under Pia Navida's fingernails, in her anus and on her right breast, which suggested a struggle, but John Stratton, senior counsel for the defence, said that even if the DNA evidence proved that Paterson had had anal sex with Pia, it didn't prove that he'd had any role in her rape or murder, or that he'd been at the scene when the crime had occurred.

Mr Stratton asked Justice Bellew to direct the jury to enter verdicts of not guilty on both charges on the grounds that 'even at its highest, the evidence was incapable of convincing the jury that my client was guilty'.

On consideration, Justice Bellew upheld the application, and instructed the jury to acquit Rodney Paterson on both charges, saying, 'Although the evidence is capable of placing the accused at the scene at the relevant time, it says nothing at all about his participation in the act which caused the deceased's death. Presence at the scene does not sustain an inference in the killing of the deceased.'

Furthermore, drawing from the forensic pathologist Dr Johan Duflou, who carried out the post-mortem on Pia Navida's body, Justice Bellew also found that there was a lack of evidence to support the Crown's case that there had been a struggle between the two, prior to her death. He commented, 'I am not satisfied that the existence of a broken rib, and the presence of the accused's DNA on the deceased's fingernails, in combination with the other matters relied upon by the Crown, sustain an inference that a struggle took place. There were no injuries suggestive of forced intercourse, nor any external injury, such as bruising.'

As for the lies Paterson had told the police, Justice Bellew said, 'While it may be that he answered questions put by the police because he did not wish to connect himself with the events surrounding the deceased's death that does not, without more, lead to the conclusion that his motivation for making such statements was realisation of guilt of either of the offences with which he has been charged. Indeed, there were statements made by the accused, both in the course of his second interview with the police and the two conversations with his partner, which were at odds with such a realisation.'

Following His Honour's direction, the jury acquitted Paterson, who walked from the court a free man.

In the meantime, Steven Isaac Matthews was in custody awaiting his sentencing, which came on 22 May 2014, when Justice Geoffrey Bellew handed down a term of imprisonment of 21 years and six months, given the 'barbaric' and 'horrendous' nature of his crime. He was given a non-parole period of 16 years and three months, which with time in custody makes him eligible for parole in November 2027.

But sadly, that doesn't bring back Pia.

15.

Butchery and Body Parts:

The Murder of Nicole Grant

'I went to the laundry and got a power saw and
dismembered her body because I was initially just
going to dispose of the body, but fearful of being
seen taking the body out of the unit.'

Neal Richardson

**Gerringong is a quaint seaside village south of Sydney, in New South
Wales. Set against a backdrop of Seven Mile Beach National Park, with
great surfing at Werri Beach, it's a haven of peace and calm, making it
a delightful tourist destination. An unlikely dumping place for a very
gruesome cargo.**

On the morning of 30 September 2010, a local man working on a locked gate at the end of Sims Road noticed a bed sheet flapping in the breeze near a lantana bush. Upon closer inspection, he saw three orange plastic garbage bags underneath. As he drew closer, a putrid smell assaulted his senses and he noticed decomposing flesh and bone in one of the ruptured bags. Thinking it could be something sinister, he contacted the local police, who arrived a short time later, together with forensic personnel and detectives, to inspect the malodorous packages.

Initially, it was thought the remains were possibly of animal origin and that some unsociable person had left the waste material under the roadside bushes. A presumptive test carried out on the bloodstained bed sheet returned a negative test for human blood, while a local veterinarian who inspected the contents of one of the bags identified one of the bones to be an animal pelvis, probably that of a young calf. However, there was some doubt about the other contents.

Later that afternoon, police contacted the Glebe mortuary and spoke to the duty pathologist, Dr Istvan Szentmariay, regarding the find. He requested that some photographs be sent for review. Unfortunately, they were sent via email, and were of such low quality he was unable to ascertain whether the remains were human or non-human. Consequently, he asked for the specimens to be taken to the mortuary for a closer examination, which confirmed they were, in fact, human. A portion of a left hand was found in a condition that still enabled fingerprints to be taken, thus making it possible to identify the victim. The poor person in question was Nicole Kirrilee Grant, a prostitute known to the police. The submitted exhibits were truly a melange, with both animal and human remains being present. Multiple plastic bags of different types contained human remains in various stages of decomposition; some were dried and others were moist. The skeletal remains showed the presence of multiple cuts on various bones, including the left and right clavicle, left and right scapula, multiple ribs, bones of both arms, bones of both legs, and the thoracic and lumbar vertebrae. A black bag containing a GMC brand power saw with human material and bone in the teeth was also present, along with a decomposing woman's head.

Nicole's body had been extensively butchered prior to disposal.

Her body parts arrived at the Glebe Department of Forensic Medicine on the morning of 1 October 2010, and the post-mortem was carried out by Dr Istvan Szentmariay over the 4th and 5th.

The entire exhibit, consisting of multiple body parts, was X-rayed, but no suspicious radio-opaque material, such as a bullet, was observed. The report on the decomposing human torso made for grim reading, and I've reproduced some of it here so you can gain some idea of the horror:

It was moist, with slippery surface and extensive adiopocere formation. Most of the remaining skin was relatively well preserved and showed normal colour. Posteriorly, the skin covered the torso to the level of the lower neck, on both sides to the level of the armpits. On the right side the skin was recognisable down to the level of the 9th rib and on the left side at around the 12th rib. Slightly above this level was a nearly vertical full thickness slit-like defect which measured 4.6 cm in length; no definite underlying wound track was identified.

There was a large linear full thickness skin defect connecting the right anterior-lower neck area to the lateral aspect of the right breast (gaping defect). The inferior border of the skin still present was the lower third of the right breast and about 10 cm below the inferior level of the left breast. A large portion of the skin of the left breast was not present (nipples could not be identified), leaving an irregularly oval shaped defect in this area, measuring up to 16 cm in largest dimension. There were three vertically arranged (on top of each other) slightly gaping defects on the superior aspect of the left breast. The underlying soft tissue was soft and decomposing; no definite wound tracks were identified. In all the described parts of the torso, the skin margins were soft, thinned and decomposing.

As for the other decomposing body parts, Dr Szentmariay reported:

Decomposing head with an attached off-white/light grey empty collapsed plastic bag along with occasional small pieces of soft tissue. The remaining relatively small amount of brain material inside the skull was in a semi liquid state; no material reminiscent of blood was noted. The content of the cranial cavity was visible through the foramen magnum. The overall weight of the specimen was 2700 g. Due to post-mortem decompositional changes, a portion of the right side of the scalp was nearly completely separated and measured 25.5 x 29 cm (flattened) with some hair still present on it (sampled and taken by police for colour and length – identification). Three small piercing holes were noted in the right earlobe. The soft tissue removed from the head weighed 660 g. The peeled, seemingly blonde hair weighed 480 g and it measured up to 25–30 cm in length.

However, he also noted that the post-mortem examination had:

… a somewhat limited value due to decompositional changes, certain tissues were not recovered and no forensically important major neck structures could be evaluated for possible injuries. There were numerous skin defects which may represent in vivo [sustained while alive] injuries along multiple defects on the anterior aspect of the liver however exact interpretation of these lesions can be difficult. Similarly, defects described above involving the anterior/inferior aspect of the liver may have been inflicted. The injury pattern of some vertebrae (cuts) suggests infliction from the front (rather than from the back). The presence of multiple blade marks on the face is rather unusual in dismemberment cases. Some cuts were described as only 1 mm in width and some as much as 6 mm, which may be a reflection of the sharp instrument(s) used.

The toxicology report revealed that a liver sample (a suitable blood sample was not available) taken at the post-mortem was found to have present codeine 0.37 milligrams per kilogram. No other drugs were detected.

The reported drug concentrations in the liver from codeine fatalities range from 0.6 to 45 mg/kg, with an average being 6.8 mg/kg. The level of the drug detected in Nicole Grant's liver (0.37 mg/kg) was far short of a fatal concentration and indicated that the drug had been ingested sometime earlier prior to death. I concluded that the level of codeine detected in Nicole Grant's liver was consistent with a moderate ingestion of the drug sometime before her death.

★

Abusive people are often very dependent upon their partners for their sense of self-esteem. While appearing to be powerful, they often feel powerless within themselves and their relationship may be the only place where they have a sense of power. By keeping their partners in a diminished, fearful or dependent state, they try to ensure that their partners are kept under control. Unfortunately for Nicole, she'd been drawn into a violent, abusive relationship with such a person – Neal Richardson. They shared a unit in Malabar, in the east of Sydney, and had an 'on and off' relationship. Their lifestyle was unusual, with Nicole working as a prostitute to supplement a pension, and their relationship was characterised by drug and alcohol abuse. But worse than that was the physical abuse that led to.

It peaked after Nicole made a statement to a Maroubra police officer on 23 October 2009, while she was in the Prince of Wales Hospital. She said that Richardson had assaulted her with a car lock, causing the severe injuries that she had, and that previously, he'd said he'd had enough of her and had grabbed her around the neck with a tartan scarf and dragged her by her leg before binding her with cable ties. At the same time, he'd shouted at her, 'That's why your sister died, you're both c★★ts.' (Nicole's twin sister had been murdered some years earlier in Brisbane.) 'Shut up, shut up. I don't want to hear you cry, this will stop you from crying.' Then he'd stuffed a sock down her throat and covered her mouth with masking tape before kneeing her in the chest and stomach. When he'd eventually fallen asleep, she'd been able to free herself by using a cigarette lighter to burn the cable ties.

She also told the police, 'I'm terrified of Neal and I don't want to go back to the unit.' Then she asked for emergency accommodation.

Richardson was subsequently charged with assaulting her occasioning her actual bodily harm in October 2009, and she was due to give evidence against him the following year, on 19 April 2010.

Unfortunately, in the meantime, she returned to the unit that she and Richardson shared, and faced further physical and mental abuse.

Shortly after midnight on 18 April, the day before she was due to give evidence against Richardson, Nicole made a number of calls to the National Australia Bank, requesting a new credit card. She appeared to be distressed.

The following day, Richardson, who had been on remand for a month after the assault charge, duly turned up at Waverly Local Court, but Nicole didn't, and the assault charge against him was dismissed. Later that same day, Richardson was observed purchasing three orange plastic bags and a shovel, and that evening, a neighbour saw him beside his car with a removalist-type trolley, the latter two items being found later by police in the boot of Richardson's car, both with blood stains that matched Nicole's DNA. Nicole was never seen alive again.

Following the discovery of Nicole's body parts in three orange plastic sacks, detectives and forensics went to work with a passion and gathered enough evidence to have Neal Richardson arrested. The matter then went before Justice Lucy McCallum in the NSW Supreme Court in Sydney on 1 November 2011.

The Crown prosecutor, Sarah Huggett, started by alleging that Neal Richardson, 45, had murdered Nicole Grant, 41, between 17 and 25 April 2010, before dismembering her body and placing the body parts into plastic garbage bags and dumping them in a paddock.

Detective Phillip Brown said he'd gone to the Gerringong property on 30 September 2010 after a neighbour had contacted the police. On arrival, he'd seen an orange bag under a large bush. The bag had contained what appeared to be a pelvis bone and a smaller black bag, which on further investigation had been found to be concealing a GMC brand power saw covered in what looked like human material and bone debris. The bag had also held a decomposing woman's head.

A crime scene officer, Mark Hollands, also provided testimony regarding the exhibits found on the Gerringong property.

Graham Turnbull SC, appearing for Neal Richardson, admitted that his client had cut up the body of Nicole Kirrilee Grant and disposed of it. But he pointed out that not only could the Crown not prove Richardson had caused her death, but that Nicole Grant had been a 'sick woman', with psychiatric problems who had been working as a prostitute for many years, and had abused alcohol and drugs.

Ms Sarah Huggett said that although the Crown could not point to Nicole's precise cause of death, Richardson had earlier been charged with assaulting her, occasioning her actual bodily harm, in October 2009, and that she'd been due to give evidence against him on 19 April 2010. She continued, saying that shortly after midnight on 18 April, Nicole had made calls, parts of which had been recorded, asking for a new key card from the National Australia Bank. 'Ms Grant sounds, at times, incoherent. That may have been because she had taken drugs or alcohol, but she could also be heard crying and in distress.'

The court heard that Richardson had also spoken to the operator, and in contrast to Nicole, had been quite calm, politely providing all the necessary information. A neighbour who had lent them her mobile phone to make the call to the bank recalled that when the phone had been returned, Nicole had 'a bloody mouth'.

The prosecutor said, 'That was the last time the deceased was seen or heard of alive.'

Graham Turnbull told the jury that Nicole's twin sister had been murdered in 1991, in Brisbane, and that had affected some of the things she'd told the police and other people. He said that through her alcohol, drug use and psychiatric condition, 'Ms Grant became someone who was explosive, belligerent, hard to handle, unreasonable and self-destructive.'

When questioned, Neal Richardson admitted using a power saw to dismember Nicole's body, but said it was after she'd fallen and fatally hit her head on a coffee table. He said that she'd been 'extremely intoxicated' after taking some tablets and had wanted to return to Kings Cross, but that he'd tried to stop her. He explained that she'd started to hit him, trying to get past to the front door, but 'I pushed her hands away from me. We both fell over and she smashed her head on the coffee table in the lounge room and she remained on the floor and she didn't move.'

He then said the sight of his girlfriend lying on the floor had caused him to become distraught and panic because of the recent assault charge against him, so he'd taken Nicole's body into the bathroom. He carried on, 'I went to the laundry and got a power saw and dismembered her body, because I was initially just going to dispose of the body, but I was fearful of being seen taking the body out of the unit.' He said that he'd started on her feet and worked his way up, cutting off pieces that would fit into the garbage bags.

Graham Turnbull asked him if he could 'still see' what he'd done. Richardson replied, 'I see it every day, several times a day. That image is instilled in my mind.'

Turnbull then asked him if he'd killed Nicole to stop her from going to court. 'No,' came the answer. 'She never had any intention of going to court.'

Richardson also told the court that Nicole had told him that her sister had been murdered in Brisbane, in 1991, and that her head had been half severed, she'd had cable ties around her hands, wire around her body and had been burned from the waist down. He said, 'She wanted me to kill her in a similar way her sister was murdered.'

Richardson was then cross-examined by Sarah Huggett regarding the dismemberment of Nicole's body. She suggested that he'd cut up her body to 'hide or disguise injuries he had inflicted on her'.

He replied that the only reason he'd cut up her body was 'to make it as small as I possibly could to fit into the garbage bags'.

However, other evidence provided by the pathologist revealed that the dismemberment had been extensive, with not only her body being cut to pieces, but her hands and even the nipples from her breasts being removed before being placed into the garbage bags. The bags had been dumped under a lantana bush because Richardson had found the ground too hard to dig.

Regarding the previous assault charge, Richardson denied influencing Nicole to not give evidence against him, telling the jury she'd told him several times she wouldn't attend.

Sarah Huggett asked, 'You didn't want to go back to jail on Monday?'

Richardson answered, 'I never once thought I was. I had no fear of that court case.'

Sarah Huggett repeated the question. 'You didn't want to go back to jail on Monday, the nineteenth?'

'Of course not.'

Richardson agreed he'd lied to the police and others about Nicole's whereabouts, saying she'd run off with a rich man from Blacktown, in order to protect himself. 'I was going to lie to every single person.'

Sarah Huggett retorted, 'I suggest you are continuing to lie in the witness box.'

'No, I'm not,' Richardson replied.

After some further discussion, the jury retired to consider their verdict. It had been three long weeks, but they needed less than two full days of deliberation to find Richardson guilty of murder by a majority verdict.

The court found that Richardson had been partly motivated to cut up Nicole's body to remove evidence of injuries he'd inflicted upon her. Justice Lucy McCullum, rejecting the argument that Nicole's body had been dismembered for transport purposes only, saying, 'Some of the parts had been cut into smaller pieces than can sensibly be explained, one foot was cut in two, a little finger and both nipples had been removed, reflecting a higher level of criminality.'

She also noted that the jury had rejected his claim that Nicole had died hitting her head on a coffee table after falling during a fight.

Turning to the mater of the phone calls to the bank, Justice McCullum found that it had been Richardson's intention to kill Nicole and that he'd forced her to make calls to the bank so he would have access to her bank account after her death. She commented, 'The recordings of those telephone calls are chilling. They reveal that Ms Grant was at times incoherent, angry, frustrated and distressed. The offender, by contrast, was calm, politely providing the information required by the bank.'

Richardson was sentenced to a maximum of 28 years, with a non-parole period of 21 years. But it wasn't quite over.

The following year, on 17 September 2013, Neal Richardson's lawyers appeared in the NSW Court of Criminal Appeal to argue against both his conviction and the sentence. Central to the appeal was the statement made by Nicole Grant to police in October 2009 and shown to the jury during the trial, in which she alleged Richardson had tied her up with cable ties, gagged and assaulted her.

Richardson's barrister, Nicole Carroll, from George Sten & Co, told the Appeal Court that the jury should not have heard about Richardson's previous assault on Nicole because it 'would amount to a miscarriage of justice'.

But the appeal judge, Justice Megan Latham, responded by saying that the trial judge, Lucy McCullum, had delivered a direction to jurors regarding the statement of evidence of violent tendencies of Richardson before they'd made their decision.

Also on the panel, Chief Judge at Common Law, Clifton Hoeben, said that the defence council at the trial hadn't objected to the statement being shown to the jury and had used it to support Richardson's explanation as to why he'd disposed of Nicole's body the way he had because he was sure 'police would believe I killed her'.

Barrister Nicole Carroll also argued that too much weight had been placed on the dismemberment of Nicole's body, resulting in a 'manifestly excessive' sentence, but Justice Clifton Hoeben commented, 'The point of distinction which the appellant sought to draw between the treatment of the deceased's corpse after death being a matter of aggravation rather than going to the seriousness of the offence, is a distinction without a difference.'

Justice Latham was even more critical, saying, 'This was, in my view, a completely unmeritorious appeal. Unfortunately, the maintenance of such appeals in this jurisdiction inevitably delays the listing of other conviction appeals with real prospects of success.'

The three appeal judges then dismissed the appeal, saying that the previous assault had been a relevant motive because Nicole Grant had been killed before she'd been due to give evidence about the offence.

With time in custody, Neal Richardson will be eligible for parole in May 2031.

16.
Almost a Murder:
The 'Romeo and Juliet' Case

'For never was a story of more woe
than this of Juliet and her Romeo.'

William Shakespeare

Samantha Holland and Joel Betts shared an apartment in Chippendale, an inner-Sydney suburb, and from the outside, they seemed to be the perfect couple. They were both well educated, pleasing on the eye – Samantha with her blonde hair and sparkling blue eyes, and Joel with his rugged, handsome, dark looks – and held down good jobs – Samantha worked as a mobile sales coordinator, while Joel had a promising future running his own communication business, having previously had a stint as a presenter on Foxtel. But behind the everyday facade, all was not what it seemed.

J oel was born and raised in Sydney. His parents separated when he was six, and he only saw his father once after the age of 10. He had a good relationship with both his mother, who worked as a medical receptionist, and brother. The family problems began when he was eight years old, around the time his mother met a builder called Walter. They got married and had two daughters, but Walter was a very violent man, and on one occasion, he stabbed Joel's mother and the police became involved. As frequently happens, she chose to stay with him even though he was violent to her and Joel.

It's impossible to know with any degree of certainty what goes on behind closed doors, but emotional abuse and domestic violence leave their marks, both mentally and physically. In spite of the abuse, Joel managed to graduate from high school in 1997, going on to Macquarie University, where he gained a bachelor's degree in commerce in 2001. He later appeared on *Australian Survivor* for 38 days.

His first relationship was with a young woman, Claudia, whom he met at high school. It lasted seven years, during which time she provided constant emotional support by coaching and encouraging him so much that she 'felt like the mother'. However, it couldn't go on, as it was wearing her out, and the relationship became an on-off affair before they finally called it a day. Every relationship has its ups and downs, but that one, with its constant support, was pivotal to Joel's life, and the break-up impacted upon future relationships – and lives.

In December 2007, Joel started dating Samantha Holland. At the time, they were both studying for degrees at Sydney University: Joel, a Masters in Cross-Cultural Communication and Samantha, a Bachelor of Liberal Studies. Joel was living in Kirribilli and Samantha in Camperdown. Finances were rather tight, so he took up Samantha's offer and moved into her unit, which she shared with three others. After a few months, he moved out and shared a flat in Randwick with Kate Roberts.

Nearly two years later, in October 2009, Joel and Samantha, feeling that the bond between them was now more solid, decided to rent one of the Waldorf Apartments in Chippen Street, Chippendale, and for a time, they shared good times and were happy.

The Waldorf Apartments in Chippen Street, Chippendale.

Then, on Thursday 25 March, just five months later, after a lengthy discussion about their relationship, Samantha decided to call it quits. She called her mother in the early hours of 26 March to give her the news and ask her to pick her up. Early the following morning, she left with a suitcase of clothes and went to stay with her family, who lived in North Richmond, on the outskirts of Sydney.

She remained in contact with Joel, with both of them bobbing up and down on the opposite ends of an emotional see-saw, although she did say to him, 'I don't know why we're both fighting so hard for something that is clearly already over.'

After a few more days, thinking the matter had been settled, Samantha set out to find suitable accommodation, moving into a house shared by Kate Mann and Tom Roth. On 9 April, Joel called her to let her know that he would be moving out of the Waldorf apartment on the weekend of 17–18 April.

'I'm organising a truck to take my things into storage next weekend. Let me know if you want me to take any of your stuff anywhere.'

'I don't think it's a good idea that we're there at the same time,' Samantha replied, 'so if you can tell me exactly when you'll be moving

147

your stuff, I can organise to move mine at a different time. I won't need to use the truck because my family has offered to help me out.'

She confirmed the arrangement the following week so as to be sure of the time when Joel wouldn't be there. Joel said, 'I'm moving my stuff on Sunday.' (18 April)

'That's fine,' Samantha replied. 'I'll move my stuff on Saturday then. What time will you be leaving the apartment?'

'I have a work function to go to by 10.30 am, so I'll be gone by then.'

'Okay, I'll get there after 10.30 am. What time will you be back?'

'No worries, I can be gone all day if you'll be at the apartment.'

In the week leading up to the weekend, Joel rang her again, this time asking whether she'd like a coffee. He wanted them to get back together and was anxious to talk to her and tell her how well they worked together. She agreed to meet him at a cafe, where they discussed various things, including her graduation at Sydney University. Inevitably, the conversation turned back to their relationship. Joel expressed his disbelief at the reason they'd broken up, but Samantha made it clear she had no intention of sharing him with another woman, as she didn't 'want to have a threesome'.

Just before they left the cafe, Samantha said, 'The question I asked in the cafe was obvious. Did you or did you not sleep with other people? You were deliberately manipulating my emotions and reactions by leaving out that information [that you slept with her]. The fact that you went so far as to tell me superfluous information … like you slept on a blow-up mattress at Michelle's place … is also an indication that you knew whether or not you had sex. That girl was an important part of the conversation, but you failed to mention that you had slept with her.'

'I haven't done anything wrong,' Joel blustered.

'You haven't done anything wrong,' Samantha retorted, 'but it puts all the other shit you were saying into perspective. Thank you for the tea, goodbye, and have a nice night.'

From that point on, Samantha decided not to respond to any contact or communication from him. However, undeterred, he kept calling – several times a day, every day, up until 16 April – and she kept ignoring him.

On the morning of Saturday 17 April, Samantha met up with her friends and had breakfast at an east Sydney cafe. Her housemate, Kate Mann, then drove her to the Waldorf apartment. It was just after 11 am. She was going to pack up her possessions and had arranged for her brother, Todd, to call around and help her move them. She took her swipe key from her handbag, nodded to the women at the front desk and rode the lift to third floor. As she pushed the apartment door open, Joel walked out of the bedroom. He hadn't stuck to the agreement.

'You weren't meant to be here,' Samantha said, her voice conveying her annoyance.

As she put her handbag down on the kitchen bench, Joel responded, 'I've been trying to contact you. I want to talk to you.'

'I know. I'm not interested in listening.'

At 12.10 pm, her brother texted to let her know he'd arrived at the apartment block. 'I'm here. Where should I park?'

Samantha texted back. 'On the street.'

At 12.23 pm, she texted again. 'Give me a couple of minutes. Joel is here. Sorry.'

That was her last authentic text.

Joel then attempted to talk her into forgiving him and resuming their relationship, only for her to remind him how he'd had multiple dates with other young women and 'had weird stuff with a girl from Lebanon'.

'What happened with Yaara was wrong by you. Can't you try and understand this from my perspective?'

'I've been trying very hard for the past 18 months to understand this from your perspective,' Samantha replied, 'and that's the only reason I'm still here. And now I'm done. The damage to our relationship has been done.'

Similar exchanges went on for some time, with Joel trying to hug Samantha on a number of occasions. Then she remembered that her brother was waiting downstairs and started to rummage through her handbag for the swipe key so she could go and let him in.

'I'm done,' she said. 'And as always, it's me that has to show the strength of my convictions, to say something and stick by it. You can't expect to tell me yes-no-yes-no and for me to be here through all of it. I'm done, it's over. I'm going downstairs to let Todd in.'

As she stepped towards the door, Joel barred her way.

'Let me past.'

Joel moved to one side, but as she turned the handle, he started stabbing her with a short vegetable knife, raining blows down on her back. Samantha spun around and started screaming, long repeated screams, but Joel continued stabbing her. As they fell to the floor, he stabbed her shoulders and the right side of her neck.

Shocked and terrified, Samantha picked herself up and ran towards the kitchen, reaching over the preparation surface to pick up her mobile phone. Joel pulled her back, grabbed the phone out of her hands and threw it across the room. He then started stabbing her in the neck. Samantha made another attempt to escape via the front door, but was thwarted again. Joel put the knife to his wrist and cut it. Then he dropped to his knees, stabbing himself in the neck before turning his attention to Samantha for a further attack.

She screamed, 'You're going to jail. Todd's downstairs and he'll know it was you.'

Kneeling by the front door, Joel said, 'We'll die here together. Then we can be together for eternity.'

Samantha gasped, 'I never knew you were this fucked up.'

Joel rolled her over onto her front and started to stab her in the back again, saying, 'You're going to die.'

Samantha tried to escape a number of times, but each time, Joel managed to overpower her, and the torture continued. She tried talking to him, reasoning with him and even threatening him, but nothing worked. Bleeding and in pain, she knew she had to weaken her attacker sufficiently so she could make another last ditch effort to escape.

'If we're going to do this together,' she said, 'I should have a turn with the knife.'

She convinced Joel to give her the weapon, which she used to stab him in the stomach, but even then he still had enough strength to stop her escaping.

'Are you ready to die yet?' he asked.

He then used her mobile phone to text her brother. 'We're looking like staying together. For now at least. I'll call you soon. Thanks for coming today bro. X.'

He also sent a message with an air of finality to Samantha's mother. 'Mum I love you.'

It was then about 1.45 pm. Joel was weakened from his injuries, so Samantha tried another strategy to get away from him. 'There's a good quote in the last Harry Potter book [*Harry Potter and the Deathly Hallows*] about dying that I want to read to you,' she said. 'Go and get it.'

As he went to fetch the book, she made good her escape. She dashed to the sliding door that led onto the balcony, released the bolt and threw the door open. Then she shot across to the railing, swung her legs over and landed on her bottom on the second-storey balcony below.

She was now covered in blood, her hair was matted and she was wearing only her underwear. She called down to a shocked couple passing by, 'Excuse me. I need your help. I've been stabbed by my boyfriend. He's still upstairs. I need you to help me.'

Some nearby workmen saw her plight and also came to the rescue, using their ladders to reach her and help her down to the pavement below. An ambulance was summoned and she was whisked away to the Royal Prince Alfred Hospital, where she underwent surgery that evening.

The police were also alerted, and they found Joel lying on the apartment floor. He, too, was admitted to the same hospital for treatment.

Samantha was found to have multiple stab wounds to her back, neck and limbs, with 20 stab wounds to her upper back and a foreign body (knife tip) in a lower back wound. She was discharged eight days later.

Joel was found to have a number of stab wounds, the most serious of which was the abdominal stab wound, necessitating surgery, during which a number of bleeding severed arteries were found and subsequently tied off. He also had several wounds to his chest and neck. He was discharged six days later and taken into custody to face court.

Prior to the matter going to trial, Samantha provided a statement that described Joel's consumption of drugs and alcohol. While the recreational use of cannabis and cocaine were mentioned, together with excessive alcohol consumption on one particular occasion, she also spoke about a drug known as DMT. The Director of Public Prosecutions wanted to know if it could have affected Joel's behaviour and to what extent its use was relevant to the offence.

I said that DMT is the abbreviated term for N, N–dimethyltryptamine or dimethyltryptamine, and is a short acting (half-life of 0.5–1.5 hours) hallucinogenic indole derivative that is structurally related to serotonin (5-hydroxytryptamine), a neurotransmitter. DMT is widely distributed throughout the plant kingdom and occurs naturally in certain South American plants, for example, *Mimosa* sp. As a drug of abuse, DMT is commonly smoked with tobacco and/or cannabis or other plant material. Doses of 50–150 milligrams are typical. Ingestion of the drug can produce hallucinations, intense visuals, euphoria, papillary dilation and hypertension (elevated blood pressure). Because the effects of DMT can be over in as little as 30 minutes, the drug has been dubbed as the 'the businessman's lunch'.

The rapid breakdown of DMT in the body is achieved by the enzyme monoamine oxidase (MAO). However, this degradation can be inhibited by various MAO inhibitors, such as harmine, harmaline and tetrahydroharmine.

So, would Joel Betts have been affected by DMT at the time of the offence?

That was a difficult question to answer, given the absence of a blood analysis result/s. However, the effects experienced with DMT are quite short and I would have expected them to have been over before the altercation. Furthermore, the CCTV showed the victim entering the building at 11.11 am, and for approximately an hour, despite earlier agreeing to not be present at the unit, the accused was there, talking to the victim. At 12.10 pm the victim's brother texted her to say he'd arrived at the apartment block and the victim texted back a message at 12.23 pm stating that Joel was present in the apartment. It would therefore appear, if the drug had previously been in his system, that sufficient time had elapsed for any effects to have dissipated.

As to what extent it had been relevant to the offence, my answer was that it was most likely not to have had any relevance at all. So I concluded that I was unable to provide an opinion as to whether DMT played any part in the offence that ensued. However, given the time elapsed and the rapid breakdown of the drug in the body, it would appear unlikely DMT was instrumental in the offence, even if it was ingested.

Joel Betts pleaded guilty to wounding with intent to murder and detain for advantage, and on 27 April 2012 he appeared before Judge Robert Toner at the Downing Centre District Court. Before a packed courtroom, Judge Toner said, 'I find that it was the offender's intention to kill Ms Holland if he could not persuade her to be with him. It was simply a matter of luck he failed.'

Yes, it could have been a tragic murder-suicide situation. Thankfully, it wasn't.

A handwritten note found by police at the scene of the stabbings had a line from a Bon Jovi song on it: 'You know I love you, but I hate you because I could never replace you.'

The note, which had been written a week earlier, showed that the crime had been planned.

Judge Toner also said that Ms Holland had, 'acquitted herself with great courage and intelligence' by convincing her former boyfriend to give her the knife so they could die together in a Romeo and Juliet type of scenario. In sentencing Betts, Judge Toner described the offences 'as of the utmost seriousness' and sentenced him to a maximum of 16 years, with a non-parole period of 11 years.

With time in custody, he would have been eligible for parole in April 2021.

In the words of the Bard:

> *These violent delights have violent ends*
> *And in their triumph die, like fire and powder*
> *which, as they kiss, consume.*
> – *Romeo and Juliet,* William Shakespeare

Fortunately, the former lover survived and was not 'consumed' in the jealous passion.

Holly Francis-Burroughs. *Source:* Facebook

17.
Tulips for Holly:
Death of a 'Wild Child'

'My candle burns at both ends.
It will not last the night,
but ah, my foes, and oh, my friends
– it gives a lovely light.'

Edna St Vincent Millay

olly Violet Francis-Burroughs was a Canadian expatriate. She was a real party girl who loved socialising and 'chilling out' with friends. Her family background was somewhat unconventional to say the least; her father was allegedly the financial head of an outlaw motorcycle gang in Canada, and when she was born, her mother was a crack cocaine addict. Holly, her brother and two sisters were abandoned by their mother when they were very young, having no contact since then.

At the age of 16, Holly migrated to Australia with her aunt, her younger brother Ray, and her sister, Bonny Francis-Carroll, and they set up home in the Sydney suburb of Narraweena. Later on, she met up with a local young man, and shortly after, they moved into an apartment together in Manly. A couple of years after that, Holly's aunt returned to Canada with Bonny. Ray followed a year later. Holly and her young man stayed in the Manly apartment for two years before taking up residence in a humble housing commission bedsitter with a kitchen and bathroom at Dora Street, North Ryde, Sydney.

This is essentially where her story begins.

Holly Violet Francis-Burroughs's humble residence at North Ryde.

Holly's unit was only a short distance from a popular watering hole, the Ranch Hotel (formerly known as El Rancho). Located in Marsfield, an area bordered by suburbs including North Ryde, Macquarie Park, Eastwood, Epping and the Ryde area, it boasts three and a half star accommodation, which is popular with Macquarie Business Park guests, local tradesmen and professionals, and people visiting Macquarie University, Macquarie Hospital and Curzon Hall. Holly frequently met up with friends for drinks and a chat there, but some of those friends were less than desirable, offering her drugs in return for sexual favours.

With her colourful background, it wasn't too surprising that she was a bit of a wild child. Unfortunately, she also loved ice (a potent form of methylamphetamine), ecstasy (MDMA), amphetamine and any other stimulant that would bring her up. She was one for burning the candle at both ends and enjoyed high-risk sex in public places with a number of different men, one of whom was special to her – Dahkota Salcedo. However, he had a lengthy police record. A bad boy, noted for violence against women, along with robbery and property offences, including breaking and entering, he had a string of offences as long as your arm.

The Ranch Hotel at North Ryde.

Holly even said to a close friend after an argument, 'I got in the middle of it and Dahkota choked me until I was unconscious.'

He was a poor choice, but Holly was apparently in love with him. She was 'the moth to his flame'. Salcedo, who was in his twenties, was about 6 foot (1.83 metres), a Pacific Islander, good looking with dark eyes and dark hair. He also lived in a housing commission area, dubbed for some odd reason 'Smurfs Village'. However, a tragic tale was about to unfold.

*

Thursday 7 June 2012 was cold and breezy. At about 9.20 am, Adam Stenberg, who lived in the same unit complex as Holly, dropped by her flat to collect the $25 owed to him. It was his third attempt to contact her that day, having previously tried at 7.30 am and 8.30 am. He'd been a little concerned at the lack of response and so decided to make a personal visit.

After knocking on Holly's door for some time, again receiving no indication that she was there, he gave the door a gentle push. It swung open with ease and he could see signs of a previous forced entry. Upon entering the unit, he saw Holly. She was fully clothed in winter attire, with track pants and a pair of laced up running shoes. A scarf was wrapped loosely around her neck and she appeared to be dozing on the bed. Adam walked over to her and immediately twigged that something wasn't quite right. She was lying in an awkward position and her eyes were half shut. She was very still and he was unable to rouse her. At that point, Adam realised she was probably dead, so he immediately contacted her close neighbours, Steven Marchant, Patricia Mitchell and Anthony Cowan, who came round to Holly's unit while Adam checked for vital signs. Unfortunately, there were none, so a 000 call was made to alert the emergency services.

An ambulance arrived at just gone 9.30 am and the officers carried out a basic examination of Holly's body, confirming that she'd died and was showing signs of rigor mortis. At about the same time, the police also appeared, and they made visual inspections, noting some unusual marks on her neck. Crime scene officers took photographs of her body and collected various exhibits.

Dr Matthew Orde, an on-call pathologist, arrived at about 3 pm and examined her body. He noted the extensive petechial haemorrhages on her face and neck and formed the opinion that Holly had been strangled. Holly was known as a chronic prescription medication abuser, together with various other illicit drugs, and whether she'd been strangled or suffered from an overdose, it appeared that her wild life had caught up with her.

Her body was taken to the Glebe Department of Forensic Medicine that afternoon, and the post-mortem was carried out by pathologist Dr Matthew Orde at 9.15 am the following morning. He observed a number of injuries, some being minor scars due to earlier feeble attempts at self-harm. But most notably, 'There was moderately intense congestion of the face and under surface of the chin. In this region there were numerous petechial and larger frank cutaneous haemorrhages. Corresponding dense petechial haemorrhages were noted over the scleral aspects of the left and right eyes and within the conjunctival recesses of the upper and lower eyelids of both eyes. There was also a dense shower of petechial haemorrhages within the inner aspects of the lips and over the external aspects of the gums.'

Additionally, 'there were prominent congestive features to the face, with numerous facial and conjunctival petechial haemorrhages, and with a neat linear lower cut-off over the neck.'

In other words, it appeared Holly had died through strangulation. A petechial haemorrhage is a small pinpoint red mark that is an indicative sign of asphyxia caused by some external means of obstructing a person's airways. Their presence quite often indicates a death by hanging, smothering or manual strangulation. The haemorrhages result when blood leaks from the tiny capillaries in the eyes, which can rupture due to increased pressure on the veins in the head when the airways are blocked. If petechial haemorrhages and facial congestion are present, there is a strong indication that asphyxia by strangulation was the cause of death. Holly showed both symptoms, and it initially looked like a clear case of murder. Curiously, the hyoid bone and laryngeal cartilages were still intact. If those had been ruptured and/or damaged, they would have provided confirmatory signs of strangulation.

But things in real life are rarely so simple. We humans are complex creatures and expected outcomes may not eventuate. In addition, there was the toxicology report to consider, and that further complicated the case.

Holly's love of drug stimulants was borne out in the report, which showed that a blood sample taken from her body at post-mortem contained amphetamine 2.6 milligrams per litre, methylamphetamine less than 0.02 milligrams per litre, delta-9-tetrahydrocannabinol (THC, the psychoactive component of cannabis) 0.006 milligrams per litre, delta-9-THC acid (the inactive breakdown product of cannabis) 0.021 milligrams per litre, diazepam 0.06 milligrams per litre, nordiazepam 0.19 milligrams per litre, oxazepam 0.04 milligrams per litre, temazepam 0.01 milligrams per litre.

The important player was the elevated level of amphetamine. The others indicated minor drug use, with cannabis and diazepam (Valium), both downers, used to treat the stimulant highs. While amphetamine (dextroamphetamine, an isomer of amphetamine) is a psychostimulant drug approved for the treatment of attention deficit hyperactivity disorder (ADHD) and narcolepsy, methylamphetamine has no approved use in Australia.

Both drugs are central nervous system (CNS) stimulants which can impair a user's faculties by altering perceptions and judgment and increasing aggressive or risk-taking behaviour during the acute phase of intoxication.

These drugs may also produce hallucinations. Following the stimulation phase, as the blood concentrations of the stimulants decrease, there may be a reactive drug-induced fatigue stage when a user's faculties can be further impaired. During this stage the user may experience drowsiness/sleepiness/fatigue, a slowing of reactions and impairment of perceptions and judgement. After ingestion, both amphetamine and methylamphetamine are rapidly distributed throughout the CNS, where they increase catecholamine activity (and serotonin activity at higher doses), thus producing their psychological effects. Amphetamine has a half-life of 7–34 hours and stays in the user's body for several days depending upon the acidity or alkalinity of their urine.

The blood concentration of methylamphetamine was low, indicating either the drug was consumed sometime earlier or that a moderate amount of the drug was ingested. However, the blood concentration of amphetamine was (well) outside the therapeutic range (0.05–0.15 mg/L) and into the lethal range and indicates a very large dosage of the drug was consumed by Ms Francis-Burroughs. Large doses of amphetamine can result in restlessness, anxiety, irritability, hyperactivity and aggressive and/or bizarre behaviour, and cerebral vasculitis, myocardial infarction, ischemic stroke and intracranial haemorrhage have been attributed to abusers of amphetamines.

Ms Francis-Burroughs's head and neck showed a number of haemorrhages including petechial and larger frank cutaneous haemorrhages, as recorded in Dr Orde's post-mortem report. Medications such as aspirin or amphetamines may also produce a petechial rash.

Dr Orde also noted that the hyoid bone and laryngeal cartilages were

Sadly, Holly was trying to sort out her life before this awful event happened.

intact. Further, amphetamines can bring about increased sensitivity to stress associated with dopaminergic changes and noradrenergic hyperactivity that may result in stress-related psychiatric disorders.

I concluded at the time that the blood concentration of amphetamine would have been a contributory factor in Ms Francis-Burroughs's death, by rendering her more susceptible to stress-related psychoactive effects, taking into account her likely high tolerance to the drug (due to her alleged long-term use of dexamphetamine).

That proved to be a controversial finding because many were convinced her death had been caused by strangulation. A 'don't-confuse-me-with-the-facts' type attitude seemed to prevail at the time, which made an impartial assessment very difficult. But I was uncertain, given Holly's background and drug habits.

The toxicology report confirmed that Holly did live life on the edge through her need for stimulants, both chemical and physical, and once done, she needed to normalise her life by taking downers such as cannabis, benzodiazepines (Valium, Serepax, etc.) and Oxycontin (a brand of oxycodone, an opiate pain reliever). It's a common way of life in the drug subculture, where stimulants are used to go harder or improve sexual and/or sporting performance, after which a depressant such as cannabis, or drugs such as the benzodiazepines or alcohol are used to reduce the stimulant's effects so users can come down and relax or sleep.

Unfortunately, Holly would take drugs regardless of how she was feeling. Whether she was sad or happy, it didn't matter, it had become a habit. Every Wednesday (her payday from Centrelink), she'd buy a few grams of cannabis and about 30 tablets of 'dexy' (dexamphetamine). Occasionally, she would also purchase drugs if someone happened to call by her bedsitter and have drugs for sale. It was said she obtained about 50 Valium tablets and about 15 oxycontin tablets a week, which she stored in an M&M mini sweet container and kept on her person at all times, even to the point that she would take it into the bathroom with her. Valium and oxycontin is a dangerous combination, which if mistakenly taken together would have ended her life before other events subsequently caught up with her. Also, every Wednesday, she would regularly take 30 to 40 'dexy' tablets, and as the drug is an upper, she wouldn't sleep for a few days.

The drug combination clearly messed with her brain chemistry, as she was said to be very happy sometimes and quite depressed at others, at one time trying to take her own life by cutting her left inner forearm with a knife. Her drug use destroyed her life, turning it into a series of uppers and downers.

And then there were the men of dubious reputation in her life, who further complicated matters. Dakohta Salcedo, his brother Brendan, and their friend, Quinn Fillipano. They would go around to her place, stay for a few hours and then leave. As she once said to a close friend, it was 'same shit, different day'. She would buy food and various people would come to her house and eat it all. As a consequence she lost a lot of weight. Sometimes she would come home and find that her front door had been kicked in and they'd be sitting in her unit watching television and using her facilities. Holly, a generous soul, was clearly being taken advantage of, and it appeared the young men wanted more than just friendship. It was a situation fraught with danger.

The tenants in the bedsitter units in Dora Street were a tight-knit community who generally looked out for one another. Holly was very popular and her unit was seen as a drop-in house where friends and acquaintances would often hang out during the day, so it came as an awful surprise when she was found dead.

The news was quickly relayed to Holly's friends, who chipped in to present floral tributes, the first being a bunch of tulips. They were followed by many other flowers, placed on the fence outside her unit. A sign was also placed on the fence. It read 'Holly 21 years old found dead in her unit on 7/6/12. Police have found no relatives of poor Holly. May justice be served.'

When police first arrived at the scene on that cold June morning, a day before Holly's 21st birthday, it wasn't immediately apparent that her death was suspicious, as there was no weapon, and few clues were found in the house apart from a used condom and satchels containing cannabis residue.

As with many of life's ironies, Holly had apparently been trying to get her life together prior to her death, indicating she was going to stop being a 'tripper junkie bitch'. Prior to that admission, her Facebook page had been filled with references to drugs.

While a number of teary-eyed friends attended her funeral, no family came forward to mourn her loss. A sad end for one so young.

Three months later, after receiving the post-mortem report, the police swung into action and set up Strike Force Arendal to investigate her death because it now appeared she *had* been murdered, with the preliminary cause of death being 'asphyxia due to compression of the neck, as a result of ligature strangulation'. The vital toxicology report was still some six weeks away.

In the meantime, detectives interviewed many of Holly's friends and associates. But as the investigation continued, one strong suspect began to emerge, and his name was Dakohta Salcedo.

Inquiries revealed that Holly had spent the early part of 6 June 2012 with her friends Patricia Mitchell and Anthony Cowan at their Herring

A tribute left for Holly, one of her favourite flowers, tulips. *Courtesy: The Weekly Times* June 2012

Road unit in Marsfield. During the afternoon, Holly had suggested to her friends that they go to the nearby Ranch Hotel. At about 6.30 pm Dakohta Salcedo had called around Holly's unit and, while there, they'd had sex. (That activity was denied by Salcedo in an interview five days later with detectives, but later DNA evidence proved overwhelming.) During that time, a storm had affected electrical power to Holly's unit, so an electrician had been called and had set about rectifying the problem. After he'd left, Holly had apparently consumed more pills from her cache and started becoming quite drug affected. At about 1 am on the morning of 7 June, Dakohta Salcedo had fallen asleep, and when he'd woken at about 3 am, he'd found Holly sitting on the floor, propped up against a lounger, giving the impression that she'd overdosed. That scenario seemed to be quite feasible in so far as it went, but didn't answer the question as to why Salcedo hadn't called for medical assistance. Something else was clearly afoot.

Further evidence, painstakingly gathered by detectives, showed that an altercation had occurred between the pair, most likely drug fuelled, resulting in the fatal outcome.

On 6 March 2013, 25-year-old Dakohta Salcedo was charged with the murder of Holly Violet Francis-Burroughs and appeared at Burwood Local Court.

In September the following year, Salcedo admitted to his mother that he'd pulled Holly's scarf when she'd tried to stop him from leaving her unit, saying, 'She just dropped. I didn't mean it. It was an accident. I didn't mean for her to die.'

Although Salcedo had a poor criminal record (he was on parole at the time of Holly's death and receiving psychiatric treatment for anger management issues toward women), and it looked as if Holly's body had been moved, the fact that the scarf was still in place, together with the level of drugs found in her blood (in particular, amphetamine) made the admission he'd made to his mother appear to be legitimate.

In August 2014, he appeared before Justice Michael Adams at the Supreme Court in King Street in Sydney to answer the charges and for the subsequent sentencing. The earlier murder charge had been withdrawn, but he'd pleaded guilty to, and been convicted of, the lesser charge of manslaughter following a trial earlier that year.

I appeared in court to provide expert evidence and said the presence of the stimulant amphetamine in Holly's blood was the main player (along with a cocktail of other drugs) in the tragic scenario, and that the drug would have increased her sensitivity to stress and episode recurrence. The 'unnecessarily violent' attack by Salcedo on his lover was sufficient to tip her over the edge, resulting in the fatality. Previously, the court had heard that Holly had been addicted to various illicit drugs for some time and had had amphetamine, methylamphetamine, cannabis and diazepam present in her body at the time of her death

The judge recognised that the cocktail of drugs would have made her more susceptible to succumbing to the pressure on her neck and said that he was satisfied that Salcedo hadn't meant to produce the 'appalling consequences'.

Before passing sentence, he further commented, 'It is one of the least culpable cases of manslaughter in my experience on the bench.'

Dakohta Salcedo was subsequently sentenced to a minimum of two years with a maximum of four years.

Was justice served that day?

It's difficult to say, so I'll leave that up to you the reader to decide.

Katrina Ploy.

18.
The Body in the Bay:
Who Killed Katrina Ploy?

'Every unpunished murder takes away something
from the security of every person's life.'
Daniel Webster

In the early hours of 18 December 2006, an abandoned dark blue Hyundai sedan, registered to Ms Katrina Jessica Ploy, was found at the north face of The Gap near Watsons Bay, Sydney. Her belongings, including a white leather hand bag, were found nearby, adjacent to the safety fence, directly in front of a sign warning of the dangers, along with a used cup of Starbucks coffee. But there was no sign of the attractive and popular Katrina Ploy. She'd last been seen alive by her parents at about 5 pm the day before, at their home in Seven Hills in north-west Sydney.

Looking north of the cliffs known as The Gap, near Watsons Bay.

A week later, on Christmas Day, her body was found at Camp Cove, a short distance from Lady Bay Beach, Sydney. Her body had apparently drifted around the bay and with subsequent wave action had washed up onto the sandstone rocks, where it was sighted by a fisherman in a boat. It's a mysterious death that up to the time of writing has remained unsolved.

Katrina Ploy was found clothed in a top and navy-blue coloured pants, the right leg of which had been rolled up as if she was planning to paddle in the surf. She'd obviously been in the seawater for some days, as there was some slippage of her skin.

A post-mortem examination of Katrina's body was carried out on 28 December 2006 and revealed no fractures or serious injuries to any part of her body, nor any internal bleeding, which is not consistent with a person falling, being pushed, or being thrown from a boat or the cliff area of The Gap at Watsons Bay. She was believed to have drowned.

A blood sample taken from the body cavity at the autopsy was found to contain 3, 4-Methylenedioxymethylamphetamine (MDMA) 0.36 milligrams per litre (mg/L) and alcohol 0.044 grams per decilitre (100 millilitres) of blood. The therapeutic range for MDMA in femoral blood is 0.10 to 0.35 mg/L, and within this range, the drug gives rise to an appealing combination of mild-to-moderate central nervous system (CNS) stimulating effects, which in turn induces feelings of empathy, emotional closeness (hence one of the street names, 'hug drug'), euphoria (hence another of the street names, ecstasy), enhanced communication ability and changes in perception. The usual street dose is between 75 and 150 milligrams, but with large doses exceeding this, amphetamine-like symptoms often predominate, including emotional lability, restlessness, increased heart rate, sweating, aggression, hyperpyrexia (elevated body temperature) and risk-taking behaviour.

However, Katrina's body was decomposing and cavity blood drug levels are not as reliable as femoral blood levels. Also, MDMA may exhibit post-mortem distribution, meaning the level detected could be higher due to tissue breakdown after death. Therefore, it was more likely her MDMA blood level at the time of death was within the therapeutic range, indicating recreational usage.

I assessed that the MDMA concentrations detected in Katrina Ploy's blood would appear to be consistent with a moderate ingestion of the drug. The presence of alcohol may be due to fermentation of glucose in her blood due to bacterial and/or fungal (yeasts) activity.

★

On 15 October 1996, when she was 19 years old, Katrina began her first job. It was as a clerk at Bellinger Instruments Pty Ltd, Rydalmere, Sydney. There, she met Nathan Shearman, fell in love and got married. They both later resigned from the company to start up a real estate business, but the marriage only lasted a short while due to ongoing domestic issues. After the divorce, Nathan made tracks for Townsville and Katrina moved into a townhouse in Seven Hills, a Sydney suburb. On 17 September 2003, she was brutally and violently assaulted by unknown persons inside her home, but nobody was arrested for the offence.

She then moved on to a residential unit in Parramatta, again living alone. On 28 January 2004, she recommenced employment at Bellinger Instruments Pty Ltd, while around the same time becoming involved with Joel Hollings from Century 21, a real estate agency in Seven Hills. They lived together for a period of time before the relationship ended in the middle of 2006. During that time, Katrina had further difficulties at her work place, where she was apparently continually sexually harassed by the business manager and other colleagues. Seeking solace from her workplace troubles, she began dating Grant Millgate, an IT specialist. Millgate sympathised with her situation, saying, 'She was traumatised by work and trying hard to get out of there. You treat someone like a piece of meat for long enough and it damages them.'

Unknown to Katrina, she'd become involved with a man who had a criminal history, which included numerous traffic offences, as well as hindering the police. But as bad as that may have been, things were about to get worse.

Katrina used to go to a gym in Sydney, and while there, she was introduced to Adam O'Brien by Stephen Black (alias Stephen Pravdacich), one of Millgate's associates. O'Brien was a former sergeant of arms for the Bandidos outlaw motorcycle group and the owner of the Tattoo Nation tattoo shop in Wentworthville in western Sydney. He had an extensive criminal history with narcotics, in particular ecstasy.

He and Katrina developed a strong friendship, and his motor vehicle was often seen outside her residential unit complex prior to her death. He was also seen getting into his car shortly before she went missing.

However, it's possible she'd been purchasing ecstasy from him as that drug turned up in her body. Katrina had also confided to her sister Tania that she wanted to get a tattoo, something Tania felt was amusing because it was so out of character for her to want to have one.

As for what Tania felt about Adam O'Brien, she said, 'If you'd asked me before, would Katrina have hung out with someone like that, I would have said "no", and it would have been a definite "no".'

But the connection between Ploy and O'Brien was very close, as witnessed by the 50 calls she made to him in the month before she disappeared.

The inquest took place from 2 to 6 August 2010 before Mr Paul McMahon, the deputy state coroner. The outpouring of grief by friends and family members during the proceedings laid testament to the fact that Katrina was a popular and much loved young woman. Mr Warwick Hunt, the counsel assisting the coroner, opened proceedings by saying it was hoped that findings could be made into the time, manner and cause of Katrina's death. 'It must be said that there remain a number of possibilities available on the current evidence.'

I attended the inquest and was asked questions about the post-mortem tests that had shown Katrina had the drug MDMA and alcohol in her system. Mr Hunt asked if I was able to say what the likelihood of someone feeling suicidal after taking that type of drug was.

I replied, 'Folks take these drugs for the feel-good [euphoric] effect, so I think suicidal feelings would have been fairly unlikely.'

A number of other witnesses, including Sydney University physics professor Rod Cross also gave evidence at the inquest, suggesting that 'it was possible that if Ms Ploy had taken a run-up to the cliff edge, she could have leapt in the water rather than onto the rocks.'

However, the minimal injuries sustained by the deceased didn't support that scenario.

According to Detective Sergeant Michael Kyneur, in a statement tendered to the court, in the two months prior to her death, Katrina had withdrawn more than $24,000 in cash from her bank account. Her boyfriend at the time, Grant Millgate, allegedly said that she'd made enquiries about having herself killed because she was unable to do it herself. But he didn't know why she'd wanted to kill herself.

Those comments appeared to be somewhat doubtful, as Sergeant Kyneur said, 'Mr Millgate has shown a reluctance to be completely frank with information he's provided to police.'

Millgate also appeared reluctant to attend court, failing to appear on two occasions, thereby prompting the counsel assisting the coroner to request a warrant for his arrest, which was approved by Paul McMahon, the deputy state coroner, who said he was satisfied that Millgate had received a subpoena and that he'd provided no excuse for his failure to appear at court. Fortunately for Millgate, he appeared the following Wednesday morning, so the arrest did not eventuate.

His evidence didn't appear to shed much light on the death of his former girlfriend, except when he said that Katrina had recently befriended a man, from then on known as Witness A, who not only had a reputation as a hit man, but who had also allegedly been supplying her with ecstasy.

On the final day of the inquest, Paul McMahon returned an open finding into Katrina's death, meaning the case isn't closed.

In summing up he said, 'I do not make a finding that Katrina's death resulted from actions taken from her intention of taking her own life. I am satisfied on the evidence that Katrina did not die as result of a fall from The Gap or endure any other 40-metre fall from any other location. There are numerous unexplained matters at this point. Some suspicion attaches to the death of Katrina.'

It was an unhappy result for her grieving family and friends, but there is someone out there who knows who did the evil deed. If you have any information that may help put this case to rest, please call Crime Stoppers on 1800 333 000.

19.
The 'Ice Man' Cometh:
The Jessica Silva Case

'Meth takes you down one of three roads:
jail, the psych ward, or death.'

Lauren Myacle

Twenty-two year old Jessica Silva and her de-facto husband, James Polkinghorne, six years her senior, had a very volatile relationship. Whether or not their Middle Eastern background had anything to do with it, I couldn't say, but it was a real love-hate affair. Their time together, which produced a child, oscillated between bouts of torrid love making and angry slanging matches – 'fire and ice' served up on a bed of smouldering emotion.

But that was nothing compared to the more deadly form of ice that entered their lives. That ice was not of the frozen watery kind, but the nasty dangerous drug, methylamphetamine, which resembles ice in its purest and most potent form. It was the formation of a dangerous trilogy.

Jessica told her friends that she'd been verbally and physically abused and that she feared for her life, as James was not only selling the drug, but also consuming it. It was a recipe for disaster and further damaged their already shaky four-year alliance. Eventually, the years of extreme domestic abuse made Jessica decide that enough was enough and she moved out of the family home and in with her parents until she could find her feet and alternative accommodation.

Unfortunately, that was not the end of the matter. Unknown to Jessica at the time, James had become a prime police suspect in a drug murder, and he started calling her, making taunts, such as, 'Jessica, do you know who I am? I'm a fucking murderer.' Something that was to become vital evidence in future court proceedings.

High on ice and increasingly paranoid and aggressive, James called her again. It was 11 May 2012, two days before Mother's Day. On that occasion, he made a threat, saying, 'I'll kill youse all. I'm telling you, I'm not fucking joking.'

Matters came to a head on Mother's Day, when at about 9 pm, James called in at Jessica's parents' address in Marrickville, turning what was supposed to be the conclusion to a friendly family celebration into something that was quite the opposite. Once again, he was high on ice, and before arriving at the house, he'd given Jessica a taste of what to expect by texting 'I hope your mother gets poisoned by the flowers that you give her and you get gang raped. If you are alive [tomorrow] I'm caving your face.'

Unsurprisingly, on his arrival, an altercation broke out between him and a couple of Silva family members, namely Jessica's brother, Miguel, and her father, Avalino, who tried to restrain him. He allegedly attacked Jessica, ripping her pants, and she ran inside the family home, where she retrieved a large kitchen knife with which to defend herself and her family members. When she returned to the scene, she grappled with James and allegedly stabbed him four or five times to the back and shoulder areas.

In spite of his mortal wounds, while struggling to get up from the road, he screamed, 'Kill! I'm gonna kill youse.' He then collapsed and died where he lay, and after the authorities had been notified and gone through the usual procedures, his body was taken to the Royal Prince Alfred Hospital. Jessica was arrested by police and later charged with his murder.

A blood sample taken from James at the post-mortem was found to have present methylamphetamine (ice) 0.21 milligrams per litre and amphetamine 0.09 milligrams per litre. The latter drug is also a metabolite of methylamphetamine and indicated that the drug had been in his body for some time. But, more importantly, the level of methylamphetamine present in his blood was well above the therapeutic or feel-good level sought by users of the drug. He'd clearly developed a tolerance to the drug, but not to its aggressive qualities. The post-mortem showed the actual cause of his death was through stabbing injuries and not from an overdose of methylamphetamine.

Jessica spent 29 weeks in the maximum-security Silverwater prison before her trial on 12 November 2014, although by the time the trial by jury in the Supreme Court began, she'd been released from prison and was out on bail.

The issue at hand was did she commit murder, manslaughter or was it self-defence? She pleaded not guilty to the charges of murder and manslaughter.

On 2 December the jury heard evidence regarding the savage, cruel and degrading domestic abuse that she'd been subjected to for years. Then on 4 December, after the prosecution had said that there were lawful ways to respond to domestic violence, the jury found her not guilty of murder but guilty of manslaughter. On hearing the verdict, Jessica collapsed in the dock. She was subsequently sentenced to 18 months in jail, although the sentence was wholly suspended by Supreme Court Justice Clifton Hoeben, who found '… the death was committed under extreme circumstances in the agony of the moment.'

However, Jessica was keen to clear her name and on 27 June 2016 she appealed to the Court of Criminal Appeal to have the manslaughter conviction overturned and her name cleared, arguing that she'd been acting in self-defence.

On 7 December, the Court of Criminal Appeal, surprisingly, overturned her conviction, although it was a non-unanimous decision. Justice Lucy McCallum stated that, 'Ms Silva can only have perceived the deceased's attack on her that evening as urgent, life-threatening and inescapable.' Subsequently, the court ordered a judgment and a verdict of acquittal to be entered.

Jessica's lawyer, Adam Houda, declared that his client had been 'emphatically cleared of any wrongdoing'.

One positive arising from the case was that it raised the profile of the issue of domestic violence. Jessica had been forced to leave James Polkinghorne because he'd been abusive and had threatened to kill her. And worse still, he'd found the safe place she'd run to. However, although she acted in self-defence, as the Crown pointed out, there were other avenues open to deal with such domestic violence, and an apprehended violence order and police intervention may well have prevented the bloodshed that resulted.

Janet Campbell (nee Fisicaro). *Source: The Sydney Morning Herald*

20.
The Wife over the Cliff Killer:
The Desmond Campbell Case

'Deception may give us what we want for the present,
but it will always take it away in the end.'

Rachel Hawthorne

This is a rather sad case where a loving, honest and trusting country woman was duped into marrying a man who was more interested in getting access to her inherited money and two properties from her late husband, rather than giving her the love, care and attention she very much deserved.

D esmond Campbell has been described as a liar, swindler, womaniser, gold-digger and, eventually, a cold-hearted killer who pushed his wife off a cliff. To add a further twist to the story, he used to be a police detective with the Victoria Police for nine years. He left the force in 1994 after having been handed a suspended two-month jail term for assault, and there was also a series of looming disciplinary matters.

Janet Fisicaro, 49, met Desmond Campbell in 2003 when he was working as a paramedic in Deniliquin (affectionately known as 'Deni') in southern New South Wales, where Janet had lived most of her life with her family. Campbell had managed to seduce a number of women before her and get them to marry him. Janet was to be his third wife. When Janet first met Des Campbell she was a widow who had lost her husband Frank Fisicaro some six years earlier. But Des Campbell had a sordid secret past.

Long before he met Janet Fisicaro, he was a disgraced Victorian drug squad officer who used violence to get confessions out of suspects and apparently planted false evidence to incriminate them. In 1994 he left the force under a cloud and moved to back to Britain, his country of birth, where he joined the British police in 1995. But while working as a constable in Surrey, he began dating a woman by the name of June Ingham, a married traffic warden. She accused him of indecent assault and the allegations were forwarded to the Crown Prosecution Service. But initially no action was taken.

He subsequently left Britain for Australia due to the implementation of a police internal disciplinary enquiry. He clearly realised they were onto his case and decided it was time to leave.

Eventually, Campbell found work within the NSW ambulance service, where he met up with Janet Fisicaro. He was working as an ambulance officer and was living beyond his means, so was regularly in debt. A romance developed after they met at Deniliquin Hospital, where Janet worked as an orderly. Using a combination of charm and deceit, he won her heart. She was besotted with Campbell. Janet had now developed a serious relationship with a truly 'bad boy'.

Unfortunately, she decided to marry Des Campbell, much against her family's approval. They didn't like him and many efforts were taken to talk her out of marrying him. They were worried that he was just after her money. How right they were.

However, Janet still went ahead and married Campbell in secret on 17 September 2004 at a charming country inn. She was a lovely bride. She wore a cream-coloured suit and had her hair done for the occasion. She carried a sheath of orchids and appeared very happy. However, the glow disappeared when the conversation turned to her absent family members.

Curiously, no-one took any photographs of the wedding. The celebrant, Jennifer Whelan later commented that the newlyweds didn't seem to spend a lot of time together and in her view, they appeared to be a 'mismatch'. It wasn't the usual joyful wedding.

The following month, Janet purchased a house in Otford near the Royal National Park, north of Wollongong, putting it in both their names. Janet continued living in Deniliquin for six months after they married and only moved to the Otford property on 18 March 2005.

In the meantime, Campbell had moved straight into the house, along with three other girlfriends that stayed with him from time to time. All this occurred without Janet's knowledge.

Janet moved from Deniliquin to Otford in March 2005, after telling her family that she had married Desmond Campbell. Six days after she moved in, Campbell arranged a camping trip to the nearby Royal National Park. Janet was a novice camper and was afraid of heights. Clearly, Campbell did not consider either of these concerns of his wife, as he pitched their tent just metres from a 50-metre cliff drop. Here was a man with a plan; and as it turned out, an evil plan.

It was a warm evening on 24 March 2005 as the couple settled down in their camping site. After a nice evening meal it was time for bed. But first, it was time to visit the 'loo'. Being in the bush, there were limited facilities, so Janet headed to what she thought was a private spot.

Little is known of what happened next, but it appears her husband followed her and carried out the deadly deed. Her dead and broken body was subsequently found at the bottom of the cliff.

Campbell used a rope to climb down a nearby gully and found her body on rocks at the base of the cliff. Flattened vegetation along with a telling footprint and several broken tree branches on the clifftop, showed Janet had made a desperate attempt to save herself. To no avail. It was a tragic ending.

Campbell rang 000, telling the operator what he believed had happened. A police rescue team arrived, along with detectives and crime scene officers who examined the area, taking photographs of the scene and Janet Fisicaro's body in its final resting place.

The rescue officers and forensic experts then abseiled down the cliff to examine Janet's body, which was winched up from the base of the cliff and taken to the local hospital for death certification and then onto the Glebe Mortuary.

What investigators found was that the tent was pitched close enough to the cliff edge for Janet to have gone over accidently, but also so close that police were suspicious and suspected foul play.

A subsequent week-long inquest was held into Janet's death before the Deputy State Coroner, Jacqueline Milledge, a former police prosecutor, whom I'd previously given evidence before in an earlier inquest for the tragic death of Dianne Brimble. (See Chapter 13)

Much of the earlier information surrounding the fatal incident was brought up as evidence during the enquiry. It soon became apparent that throughout Deniliquin, Des Campbell had a reputation for being a womaniser and was considered something of a rogue. In contrast, Janet Fisicaro was a homely, naive and devoted country lady. Yet, his courtship was kept so quiet that few were able to warn the wealthy widow as to what he was up to.

There were many other revelations to follow, including those from three former girlfriends, who described him as persuasive and manipulative, while still maintaining the appearance of a charming man.

One thing that didn't go unnoticed at the inquest was how physically similar Campbell's victims were. They were all attractive blondes in their middle years who were either widowed, divorced or just plain lonely. His perfect victims.

The first evidence came from a former girlfriend, a British woman by the name of June Ingham. She said Campbell had revealed to her that he had nothing to his name but an old Falcon car. But he begged her to come to Australia after her divorce in 2000. However, when the divorce settlement was much less than Campbell expected, June Ingham was dumped at the airport. But amazingly, he later convinced her to buy a house and put it in his name. What was she thinking? True to form, he sold the house while she was overseas and then broke up with her via a text message.

The second former girlfriend of Campbell to give evidence was Linda Rodgers. She told how Campbell spent a fortune on fine food and expensive French champagne to seduce her at an exclusive Melbourne hotel only a few months before he married Janet Fisicaro. Then, he followed up with explicit emails a month after Janet had died, asking whether Linda would go on an overseas holiday with him. It was all very inappropriate.

Linda told the court, 'He'd been wooing me and he was married to someone else. He should have been a grieving widow[er].'

She then broke down in tears, saying to the court, 'It's very humiliating. I'm very embarrassed. I'm very sorry. I'm very sorry to the family. It's terrible.'

Throughout the inquest, the witnesses in general maintained their composure and even sense of humour, despite the difficult circumstances. One instance said it all.

When June Ingham (one of Campbell's earlier girlfriends) told the court that he spent a great deal of time on the computer, she was asked by Patrick Saidi SC, counsel assisting the coroner, 'What was he doing on the computer?'

June replied with an embarrassed smile, 'He said it was banking.'

Ms Milledge then quipped, turning to the court reporter, 'That's banking with an "A".'

That comment, broke the tense atmosphere, bringing a moment of comic relief to the courtroom.

Strike Force Saltwater was subsequently formed to investigate the incident and detectives further delved into Campbell's background. What they found wasn't pretty. He was confirmed to be a well-known womaniser, swindler and gold-digger. But, to top it off, he used to be a police officer, having spent nine years with the Victoria Police Force. He subsequently left the force in 1994 with a series of disciplinary matters pending and having just been given a suspended two-month jail term for assault.

Much of this information confirmed earlier reports. But like they say in the television advertisements, but wait, there's more.

Campbell supposedly declared to a Melbourne newspaper that there was wide-scale corruption within the police service, and that it was, 'one endless roller-coaster of lies, fabrication of evidence, perjury, stealing and scams'. He went on to say, 'I was just scum. I became like the people I was arresting.'

Maybe so, but he was unrepentant and still carried on with the corruption.

He later left Victoria and returned to England, the land of his birth, where he served three years with the Surrey Police. However, he eventually resigned after being accused of sexual assault after he met a woman during a domestic violence investigation. As they say, a leopard doesn't change its spots.

Des Campbell then left Britain and took up studies to become a paramedic in Australia. He graduated and was eventually stationed as an ambulance officer in Deniliquin, NSW. It was here where he met the by then well-off widow Janet Fisicaro, a hospital orderly. Campbell courted her, won her heart and they were married.

But the matter didn't end after Janet's fatal cliff-top fall.

Campbell decided not to attend his wife's funeral and after being widowed for a week, sought a copy of Janet's will. The besotted lady had changed her will to leave him almost half of her estate with the balance to her son.

Campbell then turned his attentions to one of his earlier girlfriends, Gorica Velicanski, taking her on a holiday to Townsville. And like his previous lovers, Ms Velicanski did not know he was married. Nevertheless, he proposed to the woman, who wisely turned him down. And Janet Fisicaro was in her grave only some four days earlier!

Undeterred, Campbell turned to the internet and landed a further victim in the Philippines, a month after Janet's funeral. Her name was Melissa. She was to become Campbell's fourth victim. But, sadly, there were to be further victims in the form of two children she had with Campbell.

By now, the prosecution had enough evidence to convict Desmond Campbell.

It was a pleasant, though partly cloudy, Tuesday morning when Desmond Campbell's murder trial commenced on 13 April 2010, before Justice Megan Latham in the NSW Supreme Court in Sydney.

The crown prosecutor, Mark Tedeschi QC, started by alleging that Desmond Campbell, 52, had carefully chosen the site to dispatch his 49-year-old wife Janet saying, '... that it was a most unlikely, uncomfortable and unsafe camping spot that one could imagine'.

Desmond Campbell had previously pleaded not guilty to murder.

Mr Tedeschi stated that, 'The Crown case is that the accused's relationship with Janet Campbell, from beginning to end, was motivated by how much money he could get from her. He merely saw her as a source of large amounts of money. His marriage to her was a complete and utter sham.'

Crown Prosecutor Mark Tedeschi told the court that Mr Campbell's motive for killing his wife '... was sheer greed for money'.

The court further learned that in the weeks leading up to his marriage to Janet Fisicaro, Campbell was seeing other women and even maintained a relationship with three of them after his marriage.

Sean Hughes SC, appearing for Desmond Campbell, admitted that his client might justifiably be regarded as '... a philanderer, a womaniser, a cad and perhaps even a gold–digger. But not necessarily a murderer'.

He urged the jury not to be influenced by what they thought about the accused man, and reminded them that he had pleaded not guilty to murder.

Further evidence was provided by various forensic police officers and from Professor Rod Cross, who formed the opinion from the witness box that Janet Campbell was most likely pushed off the cliff.

Then, in May 2010, before sending the jury out to consider their verdict, Justice Latham advised them not to be swayed by sympathy for Janet Campbell, nor by the immoral activities of her new husband that had been heard as evidence had been presented. However, the judge concluded that Des Campbell's attitude towards women could 'inspire revulsion'.

Not surprisingly, the jury returned a guilty verdict. Campbell stood stony faced as the verdict was read out. Justice Latham sentenced him to a non-parole period of 24 years expiring on 9 May 2034 with a balance of nine years expiring on 9 May 2043.

Then, in early 2014, Des Campbell's legal team appealed against the conviction on four grounds which included the 'prejudicial' evidence provided by retired physics professor Rod Cross. This was remarkably similar to the appeal launched in another case, involving Gordon Wood, and Professor Cross gave evidence in both cases relating to the physics of cliff falls. April Francis, Campbell's barrister, told the NSW Court of Appeal consisting of three judges, Chief Justice Tom Bathurst, Justice Peter Hidden and Justice Carolyn Simpson, that Professor Cross's expertise was not relevant to the fall involved, as there was a shoe print of Mrs Campbell's found at the scene. She added, he wasn't an independent witness as he was engaged by the Crown.

The judges agreed that it had not been properly determined that Professor Cross had 'the relevant expertise, derived from both study and experience, to provide the expert opinions that he did'. However, they were 'satisfied beyond reasonable doubt of Mr Campbell's guilt on the evidence properly admitted at trial' and dismissed the other three grounds of the appeal. The earlier sentence stood, with Campbell's earliest release from prison dated at May 2034.

Curiously, if Des Campbell had shown some affection for his wife he may have got away with murder. But then, if it was genuine affection, he would not have carried out the foul deed anyway. Further, suspicions may not have been aroused if Campbell had turned up at his wife's funeral or waited more than a few days before seeking out the contents of her will. In addition, he may have been seen as a grieving widower had he not taken one of his several lovers on a luxurious holiday the week Janet died.

But Janet Fisicaro was besotted by Campbell and would not listen to her worried family; she was sure that she would be with Des Campbell for the rest of her life. Sadly, she had no idea how little of that life she was to enjoy.

Another trusting moth burnt in the flame of evil.

Lisa Harnum. *Source: The Sydney Morning Herald*

21.

Fifteenth Floor Fatality:
The Simon Gittany Case

'Women want a man who is in control.
But not a man who is controlling
– there's the difference.'
Jim Storm

L isa Cecilia Harnum was a Canadian expatriate, born in Toronto. She was a very attractive, vibrant young hairdresser. But her passion was dance. She studied jazz, tap and ballet and was recognised as a very promising ballerina.

Her family background was very conventional and loving. Unfortunately, she was attracted to a 'bad boy' who was anything but conventional. Initially charming, charismatic and attentive, Simon Gittany courted Lisa to the point that she accepted his marriage proposal and they were engaged to be married. Then, in early 2010, he invited her to move into his luxury rented Sydney apartment, number 1503, on the 15th floor of The Hyde building in Liverpool Street, Sydney, which offered stunning views over Hyde Park with the Opera House and Sydney Harbour in the background. A very prestigious address. And one that appeared a most unlikely backdrop for the tragedy that was to unfold.

Sadly, after a mere six weeks, Simon Gittany was to reveal his true colours as an 'emotionally abusive control freak'.

Lisa dreamed of permanent residency in Australia and shared a number of photos of Gittany in the early days of their relationship with her friends in Canada. Several showed her gazing adoringly at her older fiancé. Her friends looked at the photographs in disbelief, 'What is she doing? Who this guy? He looks 50!' In reality, Gittany was just nine years her senior, at 38 years of age.

But more was to come; now she was expected to submit and serve him. In addition, Gittany installed surveillance equipment which included three cameras within the apartment area linked to his computer and a backup hard drive located in the ceiling! The jealous and very controlling fiancé now had a system to keep Lisa Harnum under constant surveillance.

Eventually, Lisa realised what was going on and prepared a handwritten card which said, 'There are surveillance cameras inside and outside the house' to warn any of her friends who came to the apartment.

Then, just before Lisa's 29th birthday, Gittany told Lisa to quit her job at a hairdressing salon as she should be looking for 'a better class of people'. And Simon Gittany was just only getting started.

By September that year, he began cutting Lisa off from her friends, both male and female. They mysteriously disappeared from her Facebook account. Further, the couple stopped going to clubs because Gittany didn't like the attention Lisa got from other men.

On 2 October 2010 Lisa sent a text to her mother, Joan Harnum, 'I miss my family and friends so much,' adding, 'I have no life.'

But despite other happier texts, mostly to reassure her mother, Lisa was slowly, but surely, being isolated from family and friends. The once social and vivacious young woman was now being dictated about where she went, what she wore, who she spoke to, who she worked for – and how she worshipped (she was even required to convert to Catholicism, Gittany's faith).

When Gittany proposed to Lisa on her 30th birthday, he did it before an audience in a room full of his friends and family, but sadly none of hers. It was very one-sided.

Back in Toronto, Lisa's family were growing increasingly concerned as Lisa's texts showed two contrasting relationships: one apparently loving and the other suffocating and abusive.

In reality, Lisa was now becoming terrified of her fiancé and his controlling ways. But worse was yet to come.

*

Prior to meeting Simon Gittany, Lisa was in a relationship with a married man, George Karam, while studying and working at Australian Hair & Beauty in Sydney's Bondi Junction. He was also working in the hairdressing industry. Unfortunately, this affair led to tensions and arguments with her close friend and confidante, Amalia Karaeva, who soon showed her disapproval about Lisa's illicit relationship. Amalia and Lisa shared a two-bedroom apartment on Cook Road, Centennial Park. It had been more than five years since Lisa packed her gear and left Toronto, where she had been living with her mother, Joan Harnum.

It became apparent to Lisa that she needed to find another flatmate, as it was clearly impossible to move in with her paramour. In the meantime, her mother Joan came to Australia to visit her daughter for Christmas and during that time they spoke about Lisa's affair with George. She understood her daughter's attraction to the man saying, 'He was the type of guy you could easily fall for. He was very charming, made her laugh.' But more importantly, he was *married*. She then asked Lisa, 'Do you really want this? It's not a good idea.' Lisa took this onboard, and when her mother left to go back to Canada, she broke up with George. But before they severed the relationship, he introduced her to a future nightmare, Simon Gittany.

★

It was a warm morning just before dawn on Saturday 30 July 2011 when Lisa Cecilia Harnum slipped out of the bed she was sharing with her fiancé, crept quietly into the beige marble bathroom of their luxury apartment and reached for the telephone to call her mother in Toronto, some 15,558 kilometres from Sydney.

It was a call that culminated her fears about Simon Gittany, now recognised as an emotionally abusive control freak, and whom Lisa was planning to leave, along with the suffocating environment he had created for her.

'Mommy, I just want to you to know that I love you and Jason [her beloved elder brother] with all my heart.'

This call seemed so out of character for Lisa, so her concerned mother asked, 'What's wrong?'

Lisa continued now in a state of controlled panic saying, 'Mommy, if anything happens to me, please contact Michelle.' She then asked her mother to note down the details of the life coach, Michelle Richmond, whom she had been confiding in for the past three weeks, and repeatedly asked her mother to read them back to her. To which, her now very concerned mother responded, 'What the hell is going on?'

Lisa nervously responded, 'Mommy, it's okay. I'll call and talk to you as soon as I can. However, I can.'

It was the last time Joan Harnum heard from her daughter.

Unfortunately, Gittany had been listening to the conversation behind the bathroom door. As she emerged from the bathroom Lisa bolted to the front door of the apartment. A shadow passes across the hidden pinhole camera buried in the wall.

Gittany is in hot pursuit of his quarry. Lisa makes it into the hallway screaming, 'Please help me, help, God help me!' Hoping the commotion will attract the attention from the neighbours.

The poor woman has no chance as the practised bodybuilder wraps a muscled arm around her frame while his hand covers her mouth to muffle her screams. Simon Gittany then brutally hauls her back into the apartment, past a packed purple suitcase and a travel bag containing her passport to freedom.

What happened next, one can only speculate. A violent final argument perhaps? Before Gittany apparently rendered her unconscious, then picked up his petite fiancée and dropped her over the balcony like a bag of trash.

The 30-year-old Canadian woman didn't utter a sound as she plummeted to her death from the 15th floor onto the concrete pavement below, 69 seconds later at 9.55 am. Curiously, even her black handbag went with her. But, more importantly, so did her warning written on a carefully torn up kikki.K stationery card in her jeans which read, 'There are surveillance cameras inside and outside the house.' (The clever woman had left an evidence trail.)

Gittany, in the meantime, went back into the apartment with his hands placed on his head. He later put on a white T-shirt and, still wearing his red striped pyjama pants, headed off to the lift. The time is just past 9.56 am as the events are recorded by the Hyde apartments' internal security cameras.

By the time Gittany reaches his fiancée's body, she has already been attended to by a passing orthopaedic surgeon, Dr Angus Grey. Her dark hair and dark navy clothing hiding devastating injuries, which included broken ribs and a number of spinal fracture dislocations. The doctor checked for a pulse and found none, realising that the young woman was beyond saving.

Just then, Gittany finds his voice and says, 'That's my fiancée.'

The doctor and a passer-by, Ms Rae Morris, who assisted him by shielding them from the crowd of on-lookers, are astonished at how calm he is. Asking themselves, 'Why doesn't he look upset? Maybe he is in shock.'

An ambulance arrives and parks nearby. Shortly after, two police officers, from the Surry Hills Police Station arrive. The officers, Jacob Rex and Darren Paul, are directed to Simon Gittany standing in Liverpool Street. He was subsequently taken to Surry Hills Police Station to make a statement while The Hyde apartment was cordoned off as a crime scene.

Meantime, Dr Grey made his last futile attempts to resuscitate Lisa Harnum. Finally, the doctor accepts that she died from the massive trauma received from the fall from 15 floors and that he could not do anymore, other than pronounce her death.

Now the police had a confirmation of her death they could proceed with their appropriate investigations. Another police officer, Sergeant Brett Wall, arrived at the scene and spoke to Gittany. He was from the unit that investigated all deaths, which involved getting statements from witnesses and documenting details from the possible crime scene.

Surprisingly, on receiving this information Gittany drops his head into his hands and begins his charade, repeating over and over again, 'Baby, baby, baby, I can't believe it.'

It is now 10.05 am when Gittany finally gives Sergeant Wall his account of what happened just before Lisa fell to her death saying, 'She just walked out onto the balcony, she got over the rail. I said, "What are you doing?" I tried to grab her but I couldn't hold her. She was on the phone to her mother last night. It's going to break her mother's heart. She was laughing. It's like she knew it was the last conversation they would have.' And for good measure, 'It's like God knew.' It is then he admits to the intensive surveillance system inside the apartment remarking, 'I hope the cameras inside the unit worked.'

Another surprising response. When a crime scene is established, it is standard practice to source CCTV footage from various areas such as security cameras from shops and the streets, for example. However, it was unusual to have this inside the confines of an apartment. These cameras now took on a new significance; maybe now to show how the awful event unfolded.

Gittany was asked whether he would sign a consent form for the apartment to become a crime scene, rather than having to get warrant permission from a judge. He agreed and Sergeant Wall read him his rights. Simon Gittany was then escorted to a police car and taken to Surry Hills police station to make a statement. Here, Detective Sergeant David Weekes, who was appointed the officer-in-charge of the investigation, and Constable Rex took down details provided by Gittany in relation to the camera recording system and the various events that led up to Lisa Harnum's death. Gittany was then informed that he was a suspect regarding her death.

Meanwhile, on the other side of the planet in Toronto, Lisa's mother Joan couldn't reach either her beloved daughter or her very controlling fiancé. Understandably, Joan Harnum was fretting about the safety of her daughter, with her words earlier ringing in her ears saying, 'Mommy, if anything happens to me, please contact Michelle.'

She was so far away, but a mother knows if something is wrong with their child. And so it was, the awful silence was not very reassuring.

The police investigation continued at apartment 1503 with Senior Constable Eric Lim being the officer tasked with tracking Simon Gittany's surveillance equipment. What he found was a very sophisticated camera system, some barely the size of a shirt button, located around the apartment and linked into a couple of computers. It was a total surveillance control system. On the floor below at apartment 1403, Constable Adam Nayel was sent to observe the area below the balcony of 1503. On looking above, he saw one of the slats of the awning grate had become dislodged. The other grates on the apartment ledge of 1403 were undisturbed. It appeared that this grate took the first impact of Lisa's fatal fall.

Sergeant Wall directed the crime scene officers to carry out a thorough investigation of apartment 1503 gathering further evidence. It soon became apparent that Gittany was implicated in Lisa Harnum's death fall, but at that stage the police had insufficient evidence to charge him as further forensic work was required. He was subsequently, released from custody and he returned briefly to the apartment to pick up his keys and wallet before heading off to his family home in Merrylands, where his parents lived.

At 2 am the police contacted June Harnum and she was told that local police were on their way to talk to her on behalf of the New South Wales police. She was then told that her daughter had died from a fall from her apartment building.

It was an agonising call, one that no mother would ever want to hear about their child. She could only say to police that her beloved daughter said she was trying to find a way to leave Gittany, but she wasn't able to escape from the apartment. She cried, 'He killed her.'

Joan Harnum then, bravely, given the awful circumstances, arranged a hasty flight to Sydney to provide the New South Wales police with a statement to tell them as much as she knew about her daughter's dubious relationship with Simon Gittany.

In the meantime, police went about their investigations, keeping track of witnesses through a management system known as e@gle.i and fingerprint experts to examine the crime scene of the apartment 1503. Fortunately, the balcony was constructed mainly of glass and metal framing, which made the fingerprint technician's job much easier to develop the prints. In addition to a number of fingerprints that were found, some smeared, several palm prints were detected, one on a door frame. Each identifiable print was photographed as the brief of evidence was built up.

Lisa Harnum's battered body arrived at the Glebe Department of Forensic Medicine late on the morning of 30 July 2011. The post-mortem was carried out by Dr Kendall Bailey on 1 August, supervised by the state's senior pathologist, Professor Jo DuFlou. There were observed numerous fractures and splits in her bones, and in death her body height was nearly 20 centimetres shorter than in life. Fractured limbs and a broken pelvis had reduced Lisa's height. Her body was covered with lacerations and deep abrasions, along with significant internal and external bruising. Curiously, some injuries were observed that couldn't have come from the impact with the Liverpool Street pavement. Was she struck before her fatal fall from the 15th floor balcony?

The blood toxicology only revealed a therapeutic level of paracetamol (an active component of Panadol, an analgesic). However, the cause of death was quite straightforward and reported as, 'multiple blunt force injuries consistent with a fall from a height'.

Simon Gittany was still at his Merrylands family home when Detective Sergeant David Weekes was informed by the DPP that apartment 1503 was still off limits for Gittany. Realising his situation, Gittany called in legal representation, namely a Sydney criminal lawyer, Elias Tabchouri.

The legal process was now unfolding: a build-up of evidence, and a case for murder. Police were beginning to believe that Lisa Harnum did not commit suicide or somehow accidently fell over the balcony. But proof was needed to 'stitch up' the case against her fiancé. A second search was carried out in the apartment revealing two suitcases packed with female clothing. Much of it carelessly bunched up giving the appearance of being hastily packed, indicating a disorganised rush to leave the premises. The computers were further examined, which showed a small amount of footage taken in the apartment. However, the most damaging images showed Simon Gittany's arm across Lisa Harnum's face.

These images, together with a couple of witnesses who observed the unusual happenings on the 15th floor balcony, along with the torn-up note recovered from Lisa's pocket, appeared sufficient. Police believed they had enough evidence to formally arrest and detain Simon Gittany on a charge of murdering Lisa Cecilia Harnum.

Meanwhile, on 2 August 2011 Simon Gittany returned briefly to The Hyde building for the night. It had been close to four days since Lisa fell to her death. At 9.30 am the following morning when Gittany walked out of the apartment complex the police were waiting. They first introduced themselves and then declared, 'Simon Gittany, we are here to arrest you for the murder of Lisa Harnum.' He was placed in handcuffs and taken to the Surry Hills police station.

He would not return to The Hyde apartment again.

At the station he was advised that from there on anything he said or did could be used against him in evidence before the court. He chose to remain silent on the advice from his lawyer, and also refused to take part in a walk-through of the crime scene at apartment 1503.

On 20 August 2011, some 18 days after Gittany's arrest, a memorial service was held for Lisa Harnum at the Highland Memorial Home at Toronto. It was a very sad affair. All the more so as many of her Australian friends were unable to attend to pay their respects – many empty chairs.

By the time the news of Lisa's death reached her friends, it came with the allegations that her fiancé Simon was implicated, and formal proceedings had commenced at Central Local Court, some 300 metres down the road from The Hyde building.

Gittany subsequently appeared before Magistrate Julie Huber, represented by barrister David Price who explained to the court that his client was 'grieving' and that the couple had planned to get married in the near future. He admitted however, they did have 'their ups and downs'.

The police prosecutor introduced evidence that one witness in the Hyde Park building saw movement on the 15th floor balcony that was 'consistent with a push' just before Lisa Harnum fell to the pavement below.

Mr Price indicated that the witness was 200 metres away and mentioned that Gittany had been cooperative with the police during their investigations. He added that Gittany tried to save his fiancée when she stepped onto the metal platform off the balcony and fell hitting a structure on the 14th floor, before she plummeted to her death on the street below.

Given the seriousness of the charge, Magistrate Huber denied bail and ordered Simon Gittany to reappear in court on 29 September 2012.

The case was now being treated by police as a domestic homicide.

After spending just over four months in custody, Simon Gittany applied for bail in the New South Wales local court, this time before Magistrate Janet Wahlquist.

His lawyer, Elias Tabchouri, was on hand sporting a large black wheelie bag that was apparently holding bundles of legal documents. It soon became evident that the bag was to be used as a prop to support his arguments against an eyewitness Josh Rathmell's statements to the police. After a brief summary of the case, he then attacked the witness's statement as to what he saw thrown from the balcony saying, '… this is what he thinks he saw. Black luggage. He saw luggage being thrown, not a body. This is not clear evidence, in my submission.' He emphasised his point by banging the case on the heavy oak table.

It was a curious point of view. It was Lisa Harnum's body in dark clothing found on the pavement that fatal day, not smashed black luggage. Nevertheless, the strategy worked.

The Crown prosecutor, Daniel Noll, insisted that Josh Rathmell's evidence was reliable and that they had a strong case, as such the application for bail should be refused. Eventually, Magistrate Wahlquist ruled that the defence had raised some reasonable legal doubts and granted bail. However this was conditional, and Gittany had to report daily to Merrylands Police Station, surrender his passport and not approach any witnesses.

After about a year, in 2013, the prosecution and defence agreed to hold a committal hearing of evidence in the case. The matter was then set down to be heard at the Downing Centre Local Court, just across the road from the Hyde building where the tragedy took place.

Simon Gittany's committal hearing began on 7 January 2013 before Magistrate Clare Farnan and was set down for a week. He was again represented by Elias Tabchouri, along with another solicitor, Abigail Bannister, and Anthony Bellanto QC. He was certainly well prepared.

The statements by Joan Harnum and Lisa's trainer, Lisa Brown, were tendered to the court. Josh Rathmell by now was living overseas in the USA and gave his evidence via audiovisual link. Josh Rathmell said that he heard a 'deranged man's scream' and looked up to the building to see Gittany 'unloading' a large, black object over the balcony. Under further questioning by Mr Bellanto, he conceded that there could be doubts in the accuracy of what he saw as it 'was a quick flash of vision'. But he knew what he saw and would not have gone to the police if he wasn't certain that he had been an eyewitness to murder.

Mr Bellanto then said that what Mr Rathmell saw from the street below was consistent with his client's earlier assertion that he may have been trying to grab his fiancée just before she fell from the balcony.

Crown Prosecutor Daniel Noll made mention of the torn-up note referring to the presence of the surveillance cameras, the footage found and, in particular, the image apparently capturing Lisa Harnum being hauled back to the apartment before her death a short time later.

The court also heard that Lisa Harnum left no fingerprints behind, while a fingerprint and partial palm print of Simon Gittany was detected on the glass panelling and a railing by forensic fingerprint specialists.

By the end of the week, Magistrate Farnun was satisfied that she had received enough evidence through witnesses, submissions and statements to make a decision saying, 'If a jury accepted that evidence – and it appears to have some weight – it would likely be accepted that the relationship was abnormal and controlling on the accused's part.' She continued, 'If accepted, it could establish, in my view, that the accused dropped Ms Harnum from the balcony.' And she considered there was a reasonable prospect for a conviction. As such, Simon Gittany was to stand trial before the Supreme Court for the murder of Lisa Cecilia Harnum.

At the Supreme Court arraignment list, it was decided that Simon Gittany would stand trial on 21 October 2013 before Justice Lucy McCallum. It was to be a judge-only trial.

It was a sunny spring morning in Sydney as the participants in yet another human drama filed into courtroom 2 of the Darlinghurst Supreme Court complex at Taylor Square. Gittany arrived shortly before 10 am but this time accompanied by an attractive dark-haired young woman in a black dress and high white heels. His new partner was Rachelle Louise. As the couple made their way through the courtroom door, the gathering media were heard to murmur, 'She looks so much like Lisa.'

This was a new development. The judge-alone trial application included family support, but had made no mention of a new partner. It was a most curious situation.

Rachelle and Simon apparently fell in love a year before the trial in October 2012, and subsequently moved into together shortly afterwards. Now they were at court where Simon Gittany was waiting to stand trial for his former fiancée's murder.

The court proceedings began with the court officer saying to Gittany, 'Simon Gittany, you are charged with on the 30th of July 2011 that you did murder Lisa Cecilia Harnum. How say you, guilty or not guilty?'

Predictably, he replied, 'Not guilty.'

Joan Harnum, Lisa's mother, was in court with the man who allegedly murdered her daughter.

The NSW Senior Crown Prosecutor Mark Tedeschi took to the stand and began his opening address alleging the accused (Gittany) threw Lisa Harnum from the 15th floor balcony of the apartment where they were living. He then followed up with how the relationship, over about two years, became increasingly more and more controlling, with excessive possessive and dominating behaviour towards Ms Harnum. Even to the extent of changing her to a more modest, if not austere, appearance. But more importantly, how she became more isolated from family and friends. By the time of her death, with the exception of two professional people, Lisa Brown and Michelle Richmond, 'she was substantially isolated'.

Tedeschi then turned to the subject of the surveillance cameras where Lisa Harnum was constantly monitored. 'She was mystified as to how he was able to know so much about her conversations and messages.'

The situation was becoming increasingly desperate for Lisa.

She had reached the point in her life that she had to leave a suffocating relationship 'feeling trapped in a union from which she couldn't escape'. It was then she began to devise an escape strategy despite the elaborate surveillance system Gittany had installed to monitor her.

She had moved some bags of her possessions into storage and left two pillowcases of clothing with Lisa Brown to keep safe for her. Unfortunately, that afternoon, Simon Gittany read her messages and discovered her plan to leave him. Sadly, her well-planned escape from Gittany had not been secretive enough.

Mark Tedeschi then described to the court how Lisa's trusted friend, Michelle Richmond, in the escape plan, subsequently received an abusive call from Simon Gittany. The experienced counsellor said she had '… never heard anyone so enraged and out of control'. Adding he said, 'I'll fucking harm you.' Ms Richmond continued, 'He sounded like someone who was insane. It was a just a monologue of abuse.'

Further evidence was presented when Tedeschi turned to Justice McCallum and requested to tender five photographs taken from the hidden pinhole camera found in the apartment that the couple were sharing. The photographs were quite damning.

The first photograph showed Miss Harnum attempting to leave the apartment with Gittany's arm outreached towards her, with the fifth photograph showing him dragging her back towards the doorway of the apartment. All photographs showed some degree of restraint, if not violence.

Mr Tedeschi then moved onto the issue of the 15th floor balcony on that fatal day of 30 July 2011 and the virtually unrestricted access on the left side of the balcony, but, more importantly, the notable *absence* of Lisa's fingerprints on the balcony's railing.

This evidence showed that suicide was very unlikely and that Lisa climbing over a fairly high railing to fall to her death was inconsistent with the facts presented. Mr Tedeschi concludes that Simon Gittany threw Lisa Harnum from the balcony '… either with the intention of killing her or with reckless indifference to human life …'

Mr Philip Strickland SC then presented the defence's case stating, 'The relationship between Lisa Harnum and Simon Gittany was not characterised by manipulation, control and abuse as the Crown alleged.' He continued, saying the relationship between the couple was more complex than described by the Crown. It was a relationship that was loving, but also quite dysfunctional. It was a clever strategy.

He admitted Simon Gittany was a very unsuitable suitor for Lisa Harnum, but it mattered more from the defence point of view that the court did not find him a killer. Mr Strickland continued, 'They argued over a number of things, things that your honour might regard as trivial or banal or something of more importance but they patched up their relationship fairly quickly thereafter.'

Mr Strickland then proceeded to read the text messages Lisa sent to her mother where Simon Gittany had said he would give her time to consider their relationship and whether it should continue. He stressed that this is

'… not consistent with a controlling and abusive person as portrayed by the Crown who keeps Lisa in effect a prisoner in his apartment and will not countenance her leaving the relationship'. He then moved on to the apparent secret Lisa held and would not reveal to Simon: whether she had contacted chlamydia twice during their relationship or maybe '… he wondered if it might have been cancer' she was suffering.

A curious finding. A diagnosis of cancer would hardly have been kept from an intimate partner. Mr Strickland then moved on to Lisa's confidante, Michelle Richmond. He said that Gittany denied sending the 28 July text message to her and supported this by saying that Lisa expressed a similar view to Lisa Brown during a telephone call the next morning.

However, this was at odds with the evidence presented by Ms Richmond who said that on 28 July, she had received a call from Ms Harnum's phone but curiously it was silent on the other end. She told the court, 'I recognised Cecilia's [Lisa Harnum] number and rang back …' The call instead was answered by Simon Gittany who was very angry saying, 'Michelle, you fucking bitch, if you ever come in contact with Cecilia again, and I know where you live, I'll fucking harm you.'

Ms Richmond continued, saying that the next morning she received a text message from Ms Harnum's phone asking her to, 'Leave me alone and drop all my stuff off at the concierge no later than 10 am tomorrow. I wish I never met you because you ruined my life. I had everything with Simon but you brainwashed me. Simon threw me out on the street with nothing.'

She said, 'I felt that Cecilia had made her decision and it was best to follow the request in the text.' And so Ms Harnum's clothes were returned the next day.

However, Mr Strickland countered that his client had never made any threat saying, 'I want to suggest that he did not utter any threat, he didn't say "I know where you fucking live" or call you a fucking bitch or anything like that.'

Ms Richmond replied, 'I remember the night very well.'

Mr Strickland then went on to the suggested mode of Lisa Harnum's death, which supposedly occurred after a heated argument about 'a secret' she was too ashamed to tell Gittany. After Lisa headed towards the apartment door, Simon pulled her back into the apartment and closed the door. When she stopped screaming, Simon then went into the kitchen and made Lisa a hot drink and she sat on the lounge.

Mr Strickland further narrated the possible scenario, 'Simon then said to Lisa that he could not believe what she had just done, 'she needed to calm down and not do things like that again, that is screaming.'

He continued, 'Lisa then ran out onto the balcony, holding her handbag and he ran after her. By the time Simon got to the balcony, Lisa had already got over the balcony railing, her body and right leg were already on the opposite side. She then lost her footing, appeared to lose her balance and she fell onto the 15th floor awning. Simon tried to grab or reach Lisa with both arms outstretched.'

Mr Strickland then described how Simon lifted himself onto the balcony railing in an effort to save her. When she slid off that awning, hitting the 14th floor awning below, it was then Simon Gittany screamed out.

He adds, 'It is not the defence case that Lisa climbed over the balcony because she intended to kill herself.' However, Strickland did say that Lisa Harnum was a 'conflicted, complicated and confused woman … with a vulnerable personality'.

Mr Strickland then moved on to Josh Rathmell's evidence and queried whether he saw a man throw out or unload a body from the 15th floor of the apartment complex. He concluded that he did not regard Rathmell's evidence as dishonest, but unreliable, saying, 'Rathmell was not close enough to accurately see what was happening. It happened too quickly and his evidence cannot be relied upon.'

He didn't address the remarks made by Mr Tedeschi about his client's movements to and from the apartment or his extraordinary behaviour on seeing his fiancée's body. Instead he describes how his client was 'extremely distressed and in deep shock' and willingly revealed there were cameras in the apartment and was cooperative with police investigators.

Finally, Mr Strickland wound up his discourse saying, 'Your Honour, the absence of fingerprint evidence on an item or surface is not proof that a particular individual did not touch that item or surface. There are a number of smudges found on the balcony, and no fingerprints could be taken from those smudges.'

It was an impressive defence.

Then the relentless cross-examinations of the witnesses, including Simon Gittany, began firstly with Mark Tedeschi QC followed by Phillip Strickland SC.

Eventually, after a trial over four weeks from 21 October 2013, the principal factual issues facing the court were: whether Lisa Cecilia Harnum's death was caused by Simon Gittany lifting her body over the balustrade and 'unloading' her over the edge, as the Crown alleged. Or, as the defence alleged, whether she climbed over the balustrade of her own accord and possibly slipped or 'allowed herself to fall off the awning on the other side'. (The issue that she died almost instantaneously from her injuries sustained in the fall was not in dispute.)

Justice Lucy McCallum had much to consider – without the benefit of a jury. Her verdict ran to 500 extensive and thorough paragraphs. But, more importantly, her concluding verdict was that she was 'satisfied beyond reasonable doubt that Lisa Harnum's conduct was not such as could have induced an ordinary person in the position of the accused to have so far lost self-control as to have formed an intent to kill or to inflict grievous bodily harm on her'.

Further, Her Honour did not accept Simon Gittany's evidence that Lisa Harnum climbed over the balcony and then fell to her death. Also, no 'reasonable doubt about the accuracy or reliability of the evidence of Mr Rathmell' was entertained.

Justice McCallum continued, 'I cannot know exactly what happened in that apartment in the minute or so following the struggle at the door, but I think it is likely that Lisa Harnum was at some point rendered unconscious. Based on my assessment of all the evidence, I am satisfied to a point of actual persuasion and beyond reasonable doubt that the accused maintained his rage and, in that state, carried her over the balcony and unloaded her over the edge. It follows that I am satisfied beyond reasonable doubt of the elements of the offence. I find the accused guilty of the murder of Lisa Cecilia Harnum.'

It was a verdict that took more than four hours to deliver, during which Justice McCallum gave a damning description of Simon Gittany's character, finding that he was 'controlling, dominating and at times, abusive' of Lisa Harnum.

Gittany stood stock still and stony faced as the verdict was read out.

This was quite in contrast to his girlfriend, Rachelle Louise, who started to scream, 'You're wrong!' at Justice Lucy McCallum as she handed down her verdict in the Supreme Court.

Gittany's girlfriend continued to yell abuse at the judge, and was escorted from the court by a court official, in 'a flood of tears'.

Justice McCallum sentenced Simon Gittany to 26 years in jail, with a non-parole period of 18 years, for the murder of his fiancée Lisa Harnum. Her Honour added, that jailing Gittany for life would be excessive, but recognised 'he had no prospects of rehabilitation'.

Sadly, Rachelle Louise didn't realise how lucky she had been with this outcome

Outside court, Lisa Harnum's mother, Joan Harnum, said, 'There were no winners from the guilty verdict' but felt that the case should act as 'a powerful wake-up call to young women'. She continued, saying 'I worried for her [Rachelle Louise]. She reminded me of my daughter and it's good to know that she's safe. I felt for her. I feel compassion for her.' indicating that the sentence would now protect Ms Louise, a former *Underbelly* actress and model, a woman who bore a resemblance to her daughter.

I truly hope she is protected and is not tempted to contact the 'bad boy'. Another 'moth' burnt in a flame of evil, but another saved – just in time.

Ms Jovi Pilapil, *Source: The Daily Telegraph*

22.

The Tinder Killer:

The Alexander Villaluna Case

'People who feel the need to control others,
don't have control over themselves.'

Anon

This story begins in New Zealand, in Auckland and the Upper Hutt. The Upper Hutt (Maori: Orongomai) is a city in the Wellington region of the North Island. It is a beautiful city noted for its fresh air and many fun outdoor activities, and is also renowned for its parks and various recreational areas.

It was in this setting that Jovi Pilapil met Alexander Villaluna, while they were both training as nurses in the aged-care industry. They were from the Philippines and seeking a better life overseas in New Zealand.

Ms Pilapil, a divorcee who had three children from a former marriage, was initially attracted to the dapper little man and the relationship deepened to a point that she gave birth to a son in 2011. Unfortunately, from this point on Alexander Villaluna became 'very possessive and jealous' and mistreated her. It got to the point that Jovi Pilapil had very few friends, and Villaluna responded to any perceived 'transgressions' with violence, choking and punching her.

Sadly, it became a familiar tale where he was 'controlling, dominating and at times, abusive' of Jovi Pilapil. Not a great or stable relationship.

Eventually, Ms Pilapil had enough and left him in 2015, moving with her children to Sydney, Australia. Villaluna followed her and took up a nursing position at Concord Hospital. The situation did not improve with the move to Sydney. Ms Pilapil, in the meantime, had taken out an apprehended violence order (AVO) to keep him away.

Not unexpectedly, Villaluna took it very badly and began interrogating Ms Pilapil's teenage daughter and their son as to what their mother was doing, 'where she was and who she was with'. Abusive people are often very dependent upon their partners for their sense of self-esteem. While appearing to be powerful, they often feel powerless within themselves and their relationship may be the only place where they have a sense of power. By keeping their partners in a diminished, fearful or dependent state, they try to ensure that their partners are kept under control.

Unfortunately, Villaluna decided to up the ante, and the then 45-year-old bought a hunting knife and a camouflage backpack. On 12 March 2016 he emailed her saying, 'I want to fuck you up. You really fucked me big time. I am just letting you breathe because of [their son]. Please don't force me.'

Villaluna clearly meant business – very *mean* business.

In the meantime, the 39-year old Jovi Pilapil had wanted to get on with her life and started using the dating app Tinder. Through this medium she met a charming divorced 53-year-old businessman, Keith Collins, a father of four children and three stepchildren.

Sadly, this innocent gentleman was about to be caught up in a web of pure evil.

On 30 March 2016, Jovi Pilapil and Keith Collins arranged to meet for the first time at a shopping centre restaurant, the Kangnam BBQ restaurant at Hornsby in Sydney's Upper North Shore. It is a great restaurant for folk who wish to taste the best of Korean food with generous servings of platters of meat, fresh seafood, and a do-it-yourself grill. The couple had chosen wisely and were enjoying a top meal, as well as each other's company.

However, just after 9 pm, when Keith and Jovi had finished their meal, Villaluna walked into the restaurant. He was in no mood for negotiation and demanded of Mr Collins, 'What are you doing with my wife?'

Mr Collins stood up and faced Alexander Villaluna and said they were just having dinner. Unfazed, Villaluna grabbed Collins's neck as he turned to face him and began stabbing him with the hunting knife in his lower abdomen with savage underhand thrusts.

The frenzied attack continued with Ms Pilapil pleading to him, 'Stop, stop we were just having dinner!' Villaluna then turned his attention onto Ms Pilapil, grabbing her and stabbing her under the left breast and in the right arm as she tried to defend herself. Fortunately, she was able to escape further attacks by running out of the restaurant, bleeding from her wounds, and hid in an upstairs shop, where she collapsed.

As Collins was lying on the ground attempting to get to his feet, Villaluna knelt on his chest and stabbed the now dying man in the torso a further estimated five times. It was clearly a grossly cruel murderous over-reaction. And all of it caught on CCTV.

Villaluna then followed his injured ex out into the mall concourse with the knife tucked under his arm. He then, strangely, called Ms Pilapil's daughter and said, 'I think I killed the guy. I stabbed your mum.'

In the meantime, emergency services and the NSW police were notified of the incident.

Villaluna returned to the restaurant, pulled out a chair and sat by Keith Collins's dead body. A short time later the police arrived and ordered him to drop the knife, while a drawn taser was pointed at him. He was then asked, 'What has happened here?'

Villaluna answered, 'I come here, I find her with that man [pointing to the deceased], I stabbed him, and I stabbed her, my wife – maybe in the legs.'

A puzzled look crossed the policewoman's face, 'But why stab your wife?'

Villaluna replied, 'She was with that man.'

Further police arrived along with crime-scene personnel, who photographed Mr Collins's body and surrounding blood-splatted areas of the murder scene. He was pronounced dead at the scene and his bloodied body conveyed to the morgue for post-mortem examination.

Before taking Alexander Villaluna away, the police introduced themselves and then declared, 'Alexander Villaluna, we are here to arrest you for the murder of Keith Collins and grievous bodily harm to Jovi Pilapil.' He was placed in handcuffs and taken to the Hornsby Police Station for further questioning and to prepare a statement. Then he later appeared in Hornsby Local Court, where he was formally charged with murder and attempted murder, and subsequently placed in custody.

Ms Pilapil was taken to hospital by ambulance and underwent surgery for stab wounds to her right arm and to her chest, which had punctured her sternum. It had been quite a traumatic day for all concerned.

★

Alexander Villaluna stood trial before the Supreme Court for the murder of Keith Collins and for the grievous bodily harm to Jovi Pilapil. The sentencing hearing began in the Supreme Court on Friday 22 September 2017.

From the outset, Alexander Villaluna pleaded guilty to murdering Keith Collins, 53, and grievously wounding his estranged wife, Jovi Pilapil, 39, while they were enjoying a dinner date on 30 March 2016. However, the evidence for this cruel, murderous offence was quite overwhelming and the sad facts were presented before the Supreme Court. This included the CCTV footage, which showed Villaluna repeatedly stabbing Mr Collins on that fateful Friday evening.

Villaluna had made an earlier threat to Ms Pilapil warning '… she was lucky he was letting [her] breathe'. Sadly, it was Mr Collins who took his last breaths at the Kangnam restaurant in the Hornsby Westfield with his harmless Tinder date with Jovi Pilapil. It was their only first face-to-face meeting – and in a public place.

The defence barrister, Mr Angus Webb, read out Alexander Villaluna's statement which said that his first thought on being asked to apologise was, 'I can never do it because I'm still angry about what happened to me.' Then, somewhat piously, he turned to the book of Romans in the Bible and was inspired to express remorse by verses stating 'Hate what is evil. Do only what is good.'

In reality, Romans 9:12 says 'Love must be sincere. Hate what is evil; cling to what is good.'

He then continued that he committed murder because he was '… blinded by my love for her'. This statement truly flew in the face of how he treated his wife when he was married to her.

Further, Villaluna stated that, 'I spilt blood but I used to give blood.' He continued by saying, 'I had donated more than a gallon and saved lives.'

As a scientist, I found this a most curious comment. The average adult human with a weight of 68 to 82 kilograms will contain approximately 4.7 to 5.5 litres of blood. By murdering Keith Collins, Alexander Villaluna had effectively negated his 'noble blood donations'!

Villaluna concluded, 'I am really sorry for what I have done.'

Crown Prosecutor Gina O'Rourke described the comments as 'disingenuous'.

Alexander Villaluna stood trial for sentencing on 12 October 2017 before Justice Robert Beech-Jones. It was a somewhat warm and slightly steamy morning as participants in yet another gruesome trial filed into the Supreme Court complex.

The whole tragic scenario was reiterated before the court. It became apparent that Alexander Villaluna had already decided what he would do if he found his ex-wife with another man and planned accordingly: he would kill him and hurt her in such a way she would never forget.

Sadly, Villaluna achieved his objective, when he found Ms Jovi Pilapil dining with her new Tinder date, Keith Collins, at the Hornsby restaurant on 30 March 2016, his actions were 'deliberate and methodical' according to the evidence presented before Justice Robert Beech-Jones. He then described how Mr Collins was stabbed until he fell to the ground, then Villaluna dealt out the same treatment to Ms Pilapil until she fled from the restaurant. But worse, he then returned to his first victim to finish him off with further stabbings.

Justice Beech-Jones continued, 'Of all the cowardly and pitiless acts that the offender carried out on this day, this action of finishing off a dying man lying on the ground was the most heinous.'

Justice Beech-Jones also found that despite Alexander Villaluna's early plea he still displayed no remorse and blamed his victims for their fate. He further described the case as a 'textbook example' of an extreme perpetrator of domestic violence, where he believed he had ownership over his wife. Adding, 'The offender could not conceive of the possibility that she might be entitled to make her own choices about her life.'

'The offender regarded Mr Collins as simply some intruder upon his domain who he had the right to eliminate.' In addition, 'His lack of hesitation in coming across the pair dining, which was evident on the CCTV footage, was particularly disturbing.'

His Honour continued, 'He is awash with self-pity and anger borne of his sense of entitlement to control Ms Pilapil and kill anyone who came close to her.'

Justice Beech-Jones concluded, 'I am satisfied beyond reasonable doubt that the offender was not suddenly enraged to take spontaneous action but instead was simply putting into effect something he had already determined to do for some time, namely kill any man that he thought was showing a romantic interest in his ex-partner.'

Justice Robert Beech-Jones sentenced Alexander Villaluna to 40 years in jail with a non-parole period of 30 years. Villaluna will be eligible for parole on 30 March 2046.

Thankfully, in this instance justice was done. But there is always the terrible 'ripple effect' where the loss of a valued member of the community is felt. Often for many years.

Mr Keith Collins was a beloved father of his family. Mr Collins's sister, Audrey Jenkins, described her brother as having a very important life and as 'a man of destiny', citing his tireless work as club president and junior coach of the Terrigal Wamberal Sharks Rugby League, where he was a passionate supporter of young people. His work would have affected many young lives.

She also commented, 'I can't comprehend how an innocent and impromptu dinner date in a public place, where Keith didn't make any irresponsible or reckless decisions, could result in in him being killed.'

Mr Collins's son, Thomas Collins, not only had the awful task of identifying his father's body, but also had to wind up his father's packaging business as the driving force was now gone.

He said, 'I was forced to liquidate the company which led to dozens of people losing their jobs and losing my father's life's work.'

Another 'moth' singed in a flame of evil, but another life snuffed out prematurely

23.
The Baseball Bat Brute:
The Glenn Cable Case

'The time when domestic violence is the most lethal
is when the person is trying to leave the situation.'

Julie Johnston

While I wasn't personally involved in this case, I felt this story
was a very important inclusion in the series, as it involves a
very brave woman who survived against all the odds.

Simone O'Brien was a 36-year-old brunette, a Brisbane mother of three
children who was looking for a stable relationship after being separated
from the biological father of her children. It was natural yearning, given
it had just been herself and the children for several years.

Simone came from a family background that was very conventional
and loving. She married Trevor O'Brien and had three beautiful children,
Gabby, Ashlyn and Zach. As is often the case, pressures can creep into the
best of marriages from a variety of sources, and so the couple decided
to separate.

Four years had passed and Simone felt it was now time to form another
relationship. She looked online and clicked on the profile of a real estate
agent named Glenn Matthew Cable.

It appeared a good match. As a real estate agent, Simone thought Cable was a 'safe' match as she knew police checks were necessary to get a licence for that type of occupation. So Simone O'Brien and Glenn Cable's relationship slowly but gradually grew.

Her youngest child, Zach, was delighted that he now had someone to play ball with and considered him to be a 'gentle giant'.

It soon became evident that he was anything but a gentle giant, as he started to show deceitful and controlling tendencies, stealing money and also deleting Simone's numbers to her friends and colleagues from her phone. As Simone stated sometime later, when they began dating a number of 'little red flags grew'.

Initially, charming and attentive, Glenn Cable sent Simone flowers to her work on many occasions and eventually proposed to her in front of her children, most likely in an effort to force her to accept his marriage proposal. She hesitantly accept his proposal, as she was uneasy about the relationship. The relationship was to only last nine months, with the worst yet to come.

Initially, Glenn Cable had given Simone O'Brien the impression that he was well-off, with various properties around New South Wales. This appeared to be further endorsed with the purchase of a jet-ski, claims that he had made deposits on expensive cars, luxury items such as handbags and even putting a deposit on a new house that they planned to move into and share together.

On the surface, Glenn and Simone were a happy couple. He was affectionate and from time to time gave her gifts, promising his fiancée dinner dates and handbags. But despite these open displays of affection Simone was quite unhappy with how things were evolving and struggled to find a way out of the relationship with Glenn Cable.

Further, the jet-ski purchase turned out to be deceitful, and he had reneged on the $30,000 deposit he had supposedly paid.

In addition, money was being transferred out of Simone's account, the messages and contacts on her phone were being deleted and, sadly, she was blaming her son for losing his technology and games. It turned out that Cable was taking them and selling them!

To cap the deceit, just days before Simone and Glenn were to move into their new property, she took a phone call from a real estate agent which revealed there was no deposit (the dodgy cheque had bounced) and there would be no new home to move into with her family.

Her suspicions were confirmed. It had all been a sham.

On the evening of Tuesday 25 September 2012 Simone O'Brien was bracing herself to break off her engagement with Glenn Cable. She was tiring of Cable's controlling behaviour, and her suspicions that something wasn't quite right were increasing. She then decided enough was enough and sent him a text to swiftly break things off.

She felt it was a huge relief to end the relationship. Unfortunately, the rejection provoked a terrible monster within Glenn Cable. An evening of brutal terror was about to begin.

That evening Cable drove over to Simone's house in Carseldine, Brisbane, which she shared with her three children, and stormed inside. He clearly was in no mood for negotiation and would not take no for an answer.

Unfortunately, Simone ushered him into the bedroom in an effort to reason with her now ex. Unbeknown to Simone, it is quite likely Cable suspected the relationship was in trouble as a result of his dubious dealings and had placed a baseball bat under her bed. It was the worst possible place to take the brute.

He reached under the bed and grabbed the bat, launching into the first of a series of savage and vicious blows to the defenceless woman. Simone tried to defend herself, resulting in her left arm being broken in two places. The beatings continued on the helpless woman as she lay on the floor. It was relentless cruelty. An estimated 45 to 49 blows were then rained down on her head and face. Causing unspeakable damage to her body and face, and worse, witnessed by her three children. Gabby and Ashlyn, then aged 15 and 11, tried to intervene while a 24-year-old boarder living with the family, Darrell Millard, also tried to intervene but was warded off by the brutal Cable swinging the by then very bloodied baseball bat.

Fortunately, Simone's neighbours Julius and Donny, two heftily built guys, were alerted to the screams of the children and heroically intervened and overpowered Cable, who was restrained until police arrived. Glenn Cable was then escorted to a police car and taken to Brisbane City Police Station to make a statement and subsequently remanded into custody for inflicting grievous bodily harm to an individual.

In the meantime, Gabby, Simone's eldest daughter had called the ambulance at 6.16 pm. The youngest child, Zac, started vomiting and crying out in the corridor outside the bedroom saying, 'That's not my mummy in there.' Another neighbour, Karen Roper, had the unenviable task of holding Simone's shattered skull together while they anxiously waited for the ambulance and paramedics to arrive. The paramedics were shocked at what they saw, describing her injuries as the worst they'd ever seen.

Fortunately, Simone doesn't remember much after the first savage blow, which most likely knocked her unconscious, and in a way that saved her from the extreme pain from the subsequent attacks.

At the hospital the seriousness of her injuries became very apparent. Simone's left arm had been broken in two places and her head had been so badly damaged that her brain had been exposed and top jaw had been smashed. This was bad enough. But in addition, her nose was so damaged that she had permanently lost her sense of smell. Her right cheekbone was broken along with both eye sockets and she was left blind in her right eye.

So much damage had been inflicted on the defenceless petite woman in only 10 minutes.

Surgeons faced the daunting task of repairing what they could and saving her life. Simone was placed in an induced coma and spent a month fighting for her life in intensive care before being transferred to the brain injury rehabilitation unit where titanium plates were used to repair her skull. Her face was rebuilt and there were numerous skin grafts to repair the damage.

*

Despite her horrifying near-death injuries, Simone O'Brien achieved a remarkable outcome: she survived after the savage attack and numerous surgeries that followed and, almost two years later, she sat in court to hear the sentencing of Glenn Cable for her attempted murder.

On 14 April 2014 the trial by jury in the Supreme Court of Queensland began before Justice Rosslyn Atkinson. Evidence was presented about how Glenn Cable presented himself as a well-off with a number of properties in New South Wales, along with a number of expensive purchases that included a jet-ski, expensive cars and a power boat. However, the facade started to fall apart when Cable claimed to have made a deposit on a new house which he planned to purchase and move into with Simone. A phone call from the real estate agent confirmed her worst fears. There was no deposit and they would not be moving into a new house.

When Cable was challenged about his deceit, which brought about the end of their relationship, it precipitated the avalanche of cruelty on the defenceless woman. Worst, the savage attack that left her with terrible injuries took place in front of her terrified teenaged daughters.

In sentencing Cable Justice Atkinson said, 'You inflicted unspeakable violence on this woman and some of the things that make it worse, that exacerbate it, it's not just the injuries she suffered, and I'll go through that shortly, but the circumstances in which you did it: in her home; in spite and in the face of her desire to end the relationship with you; and then, in front of her children, the two girls who ran into that room to try and protect their mother, which was a very brave thing for them to do. Their first reaction was to protect their mother.

'But you continued the attack in front of those two vulnerable children. So they have to live with that for the rest of their lives, what they saw that night.'

Her Honour continued, 'You then continued the attack, notwithstanding that the young boarder who was at the house, tried very bravely and very courageously to get you to stop. You still continued. It was only by the fortunate intervention of the two huge men who lived next door that you were stopped. Perhaps you'd already decided to stop because you thought you had killed her, and you very nearly did. As well as the heroic and courageous efforts of her children and the boarder and her daughter's friend to try to get you to stop, there were then the heroic efforts of the

Queensland Ambulance Service and, in particular, Dr Rashford, to save Simone O'Brien's life.'

Justice Atkinson further adding, 'But since then, of course, she has had to undergo a lot of suffering in order to get any kind of physical and psychological health back. And she's been left with permanent disfiguring injuries to her face and head and her arm, but also, of course to her sense of psychological wellbeing and to the family and their sense of safety and psychological wellbeing.'

Her Honour continued, 'You rained multiple blows with a baseball bat upon this poor woman who was half your weight and only 156 to 160 centimetres tall, compared to you, a man of over six foot (183 centimetres) tall.'

The judge went on to describe the extensive medical details of Simone O'Brien's injuries, before sentencing Glenn Cable to two years imprisonment on fraud charges (associated with the jet-ski purchase along with other dubious dealings) to be served cumulatively and more importantly, with a 15-year imprisonment term for attempted murder.

It looked like the matter was over and that some form of justice had prevailed. However, two years later, it was a warm, sunny morning, on Monday 1 February 2016 when Glenn Cable appeared in the Court of Appeal in Brisbane seeking to have his attempted murder conviction overturned. He was represented by Mr Simon Lewis who argued that, 'a miscarriage of justice occurred because of imprudent advice'.

Cable said that his previous legal team had convinced him to plead guilty to grievous bodily harm before his trial in April 2014 that had 'ruined his self-defence claim'.

Cable told the court that, 'It was never discussed that if I plead guilty to grievous bodily harm that would affect my self-defence case.'

Self-defence?

As the jury and Justice Rosslyn Atkinson found earlier, he was found to have carried out a very brutal act on a '... poor woman who was half your weight and only 156 to 160 centimetres tall, compared to you, a man of over six foot (183 centimetres) tall.'

The Crown prosecutor, Ms Sarah Farndon said there was no need for a retrial, as the jury had reached its guilty verdict based on other evidence. This included Ms O'Brien's children witnessing Cable bashing her with the baseball bat and begging him to stop the onslaught and the fact Ms O'Brien tried to get away from him. Details of the vicious assault were reiterated before the court with Ms Fardon concluding, 'The evidence demonstrates that there was no prospect of self-defence.'

The Court of Appeal reserved the earlier decision and Glenn Cable was led away to complete his sentence.

Glenn Cable's earliest date for parole will be 24 March 2025.

He was luckier than he realised; the sheer brutality of the offence could have attracted a much longer sentence.

Postscript: At the time of writing (2020) it has been just over seven years and Simone O'Brien is still recovering from her injuries and had her last operation last year. Happily, during her recovery, her former husband provided her with much needed support and the couple reunited after being divorced for six years.

Hannah Clarke (Baxter) *Courtesy:* Nine News

24.

The Fiery Fiend:

A Case of Familicide

'It's incredibly dangerous to leave an abuser, because
the final step in the domestic violence pattern is:
kill her.'

Leslie Morgan Steiner

Hannah Clarke was a very fit 31-year-old brunette Brisbane mother of three beautiful children: Aaliyah, six, Laianah, four, and Trey, three. She had met her husband, the New Zealand-born Rowan Baxter, who was 11 years her senior, in 2009 when she was only 19. She was smitten by the ruggedly handsome ex-rugby league player and he by her beautiful, fit appearance and pleasant personality.

He proposed to Ms Clarke in 2011 and she eagerly accepted. They were married a year later in Kingscliff, a delightful coastal town just south of Tweed Heads, in the Northern Rivers region of New South Wales. The start of a beautiful union, or so it seemed.

The couple then moved further north and set up home in Camp Hill, an eastern suburb in Brisbane, Queensland. There are many public parks with play equipment for children, BBQ facilities, sports fields and a number of bushwalking tracks where native wildlife, such as swamp wallabies and koalas are observed. All in all a pleasant Australian

suburb to raise a family in a peaceful environment. It was in this setting that a horrifying case of familicide was to unfold.

Hannah Clarke came from a family background that was very conventional and loving. After she married Rowan Baxter they had three beautiful children, Aaliyah, Laianah and Trey. But soon after the children were born, strains started to appear. Sadly, friends and neighbours watched helplessly as the relationship fell apart. Rowan Baxter began to be emotionally, sexually and financially abusive of Hannah. In addition, Baxter controlled every aspect of her life and had even monitored her phone and left various recording devices around their house to record her conversations. In addition, she wasn't allowed to wear shorts or walk off a beach in a bikini. She was required to cover up. A familiar controlling strategy, as described in earlier chapters.

It was beginning to be too much for the gentle Hannah, who hated the controlling atmosphere that Rowan had generated within the family and even commented to a friend that he was 'so obsessed with her it was scary'. It had become a too familiar tale of abuse. In desperation, she sought a divorce.

During the mandatory period of separation, Hannah Clarke left Rowan Baxter in the latter part of 2019, taking their three children with her and the Capalaba fitness business they ran together closed down.

Rowan Baxter who was living alone in their family home and no doubt seething over how things had eventuated, started to display 'increasingly frightening behaviour' as described by neighbours.

In the meantime, Hannah sought to ease the situation and offered access to the children three days one week and four the next in the custody arrangement. All up, Rowan Baxter was allowed 165 days of custody a year of his three children – a very generous offer. Given the circumstances, it was considered a very good offer, even by Rowan Baxter's own lawyer.

Amazingly, Baxter refused to sign the consent order and didn't even consider mediation. However, he did sign a parenting agreement that gave him the same level of access to the children but was not legally binding.

Prior to this, Ms Clarke applied for a domestic violence order (DVO) against her husband after he apparently kidnapped their daughter Laianah on Boxing Day in 2019 and kept her from her family for four days. He lost access to the children in early February 2020 when police charged him with breaching the DVO after an alleged assault on his estranged wife.

Here was now a very angry, controlling man with a fiery temper, and worse, a grudge to settle. A very deadly combination.

Then the stalking began. Baxter started following Hannah Clarke and photographing her movements. On one of their meetings, Hannah Clarke noticed photographs of herself at various engagements in his car. Not surprisingly, she challenged him about it and he suddenly became quite angry and tried to break her wrist. In the meantime, Baxter applied for a position as a fitness instructor at training centre in Brisbane, CrossFit, owned by Garath Davies, where Hannah Clarke worked out. She had only recently started at the gym to escape Baxter. Naturally enough, she was distraught to learn that her estranged husband was possibly going to be working there. However, when the gym found out that Rowan Baxter had a further domestic violence order against him, he was rejected.

The stage was now set for the final confrontation.

On the fateful sunny morning of 19 February 2020 at about 8.30 am Hannah Baxter was on a school run to drop off her three children: Aaliyah, six, at primary school and Laianah, four, and Trey, three, at pre-school. The car was parked in Raven Street in Brisbane's Camp Hill when the vengeful Baxter struck. He had come prepared with a jerry can of petrol purchased from a nearby service station.

According to witnesses at the time, Rowan Baxter then carried out his unspeakably evil act. He doused his three restrained children in the back of the vehicle with the accelerant and set them on fire. Decent bystanders sought to help thinking it was just a horrible accident, but were surprised at Baxter's reaction, yelling at them to stop assisting.

'He was protesting to stop us from putting it out,' said one brave resident as he tried to get to the burning car. 'He was so angry and just going absolutely crazy.'

Rowan Baxter then drew a knife and stabbed himself, collapsing on the pavement. He was declared dead on site after emergency crews tried to revive him.

In the meantime, Hannah had tried desperately to save her beloved children but was also doused in petrol, being very badly burnt in the process, and was rolling on the footpath in flames when paramedics arrived. She was rushed to hospital suffering over 90 per cent burns to her body, but later died of her awful injuries. The three children, were dead inside the still burning vehicle when police arrived. It was truly a horrific sight.

The outcome of this awful event was an outpouring of grief and anger over the failure of various authorities involved with the nation's domestic violence system that was supposed to protect families. However, given the circumstances, I am at a loss at how the authorities could have prevented this awful tragedy: Baxter had received at least two DVOs.

The murdered mother's sister-in-law Stacey Roberts said Hannah's parents had 'exhausted themselves' trying to 'help Hannah escape this monster' and asked for donations to help cover funeral costs via a fundraiser set up overnight.

Ms Roberts wrote on her fundraising page, 'As you may be aware my beautiful sister-in-law and my nieces and nephew had their lives taken by a disgusting human being they called their father.' She continued on with this passionate plea, 'For all those who knew Hannah or had even just met her once would know how much of a beautiful soul she was, her children were her life. All she ever wanted was happiness. Her children were only a reflection of her. Gorgeous, happy kids who held a massive piece in my heart and I'm sure many others because that's exactly what they were like.' With a heart rending conclusion, 'We will miss them all more than anything.'

She was successful in raising more than $5000 within hours of going online. No wonder: all decent parents want the same for their children.

Hannah Clarke and her three beautiful children were laid to rest in a single shared coffin.

The Prime Minister, Scott Morrison and Queensland Premier, Annastacia Palaszczuk along with hundreds of others gathered to pay respects to a family that had been brutally murdered.

Ms Fiona Cunningham, a close family friend, opened the service, saying it was a time to 'celebrate Hannah and her children's lives and honour their memory.' She further continued, 'We're navigating the grief of losing this family under horrific circumstances. It's their deaths that have brought us together, but it's their lives we're here to remember.'

Ms Cunningham concluded, 'This is an occasion for sorrow, but may the occasion not be wasted trying to make sense of why we are here, but rather may it be one where we are thankful for the gift of life and that our lives intersected theirs.'

It was a beautiful eulogy – and the tributes continued. A number of other speakers rose and gave their words of comfort to the family, as well as Hannah's brother, Nat Clarke, who described his sister as, 'One of the greatest mums to walk this Earth.'

Further adding, 'With brown hair and brown eyes, after you were born Dad heard "Brown Eyed Girl" by Van Morrison on the radio on the way home and forever this would be his song for you.

'We were always there for each other. We had the type of bond that parents want for their kids. There's too many great stories to tell about you Han, we got to share so many beautiful moments together. It kills me Han that there were years we didn't talk, but I understand that now.'

Nat Clarke's emotional eulogy continued, 'I just wished I tried harder to connect with you during those times, but I'm so grateful we got the last six months with you and the kids. 2020 was going to be the best year. Han, you were looking forward to finally being happy. I only wish there was more time. I'm so sorry I couldn't protect you Hannah, Aaliyah, Laianah and Trey.'

A lovely tribute among the many that were given during the ceremony for a lady who would light up a room with her smile. A treasure.

During the services a number of children placed pretty butterfly stickers on the white coffin. Family and friends then gathered around for a private wake after the service to celebrate the lives of the four victims of this terrible tragedy.

Ms Angela Lynch, Chief Executive of Women's Legal Service, Queensland, at the time of writing (2020) said that the situation surrounding Rowan Baxter's offending was still being investigated but, unfortunately, too often breaches of protection orders were not taken seriously enough by police.

Epilogue

These stories tell just a few of the many hundreds of domestic violence and murder cases that have occurred in Australia and overseas and how it has become something of an epidemic, even in today's enlightened world.

Unfortunately, domestic violence is still said to be the biggest cause of death, ill health and disabilities in women from their mid-teens to their late forties and is the main cause of homelessness for women and their children.

These stories are dedicated to all the victims and survivors of domestic violence. Anyone in a domestic violence situation and needing support, contact 1800 RESPECT on 1800 737 732 (Australia) or 0800 456 450 (New Zealand).

Acknowledgements

My thanks to my publisher, Lesley Pagett, project editor, Liz Hardy, and production director, Arlene Gippert for their skills and understanding, along with the excellent team at New Holland Publishers.

References & Further Reading

Chapter 1

Watson, E. R. (1922) *The Trial of George Joseph Smith*, William Hodge and Company, London.

Block, B. P. & Hostettler, J. (2002) *Famous Cases: Nine Trials that Changed the Law*, Waterside Press, pp. 225–230.

Dinenage, F. (2007) *Murder Casebook: Brides in the Bath*, Sutton Publishing, Kent State University.

Robins, J. (2010) *The Magnificent Spilsbury and the Case of the Brides in the Bath*, John Murray.

Shattock, M. J. & Tipton, M. J. (2012) 'Autonomic conflict: a different way to die during cold water immersion?' *J. Physiol.*, 590 (14): 3219–3230.

Chapter 2

'Is Missing Mamie Stuart Alive in India?' (1923) *The Daily Mirror.*

'Skeleton found in a Gower mine-shaft – Disappearance of woman in 1919', *South Wales Evening Post*, 6 November 1961.

Records of Metropolitan Police: MEPO 2/8774 (1950–1961) 'Murder of Mamie Stuart by George Shotton at Caswell Bay, Glam. in 1919. Metropolitan Police enquiries in 1950 and on finding of the skeleton in 1961', The National Archives, Kew.

Evans, C. (1996) *The Casebook of Forensic Detection: How Science Solved 100 of the World's Most Baffling Crimes,* John Wiley & Sons.

Chapter 3

Fretts, B., '*Sons of Anarchy*'s Tommy Flanagan on Those Facial Scars, This Final Season and Chibs', *Vulture*, 12 November 2014.

Arlidge, J., 'City Slicker Glasgow', *The Independent*, 24 April 1995.

Harnisch, L., 'A Slaying Cloaked in Mystery and Myths', *Los Angeles Times*, 6 January 1997.

'Girl Torture Slaying Victim Identified by Examiner, FBI', *Los Angeles Herald Examiner*, 17 January 1947.

'Sex Fiend Slaying Victim Identified by Fingerprint Records of FBI', *Los Angeles Times* 17 January 1947.

'A Grand Jury Sifts Unsolved "Black Dahlia" Type Murders' *Madera Daily News-Tribune*. no. 55, 7 September 1949.

'Werewolf Strikes Again! Kills L.A. Woman, Writes B.D. on Her Body', *Los Angeles Herald–Express,* 10 February 1947.

Nightingale, S., 'Black Dahlia: Author Claims to Have Found 1947 Killer', *Los Angeles Herald Examiner,* 17 January 1982.

Carter, C., 'Tortured, hacked in half and drained of blood: Horrific "Black Dahlia" murder mystery is finally "solved" 70 years on', *Daily Mirror,* 14 September 2017.

Chapter 4

Border Morning Mail, September 1934, January 1938, April 1939, 13 January 1941, 7–10 November 1941, 10 December 1942, April 1943, April–June 1944.

The Argus (Melbourne), 3 September 1934; 7, 28, 29 March; 1, 14 July 1944; 23 August 1948.

'The Pyjama Murder Deepens' *The Herald* 1939.

'Albury Pyjama Girl: Sensational Sequel to Mystery of a Decade' *Truth*, Melbourne, 11 March 1944.

'The Pyjama Girl Murder', *The Daily Telegraph,* 5 November 2015.

A more complete version of this story is provided the 2004 book titled: *The Pyjama Girl Mystery: A True Story of Murder, Obsession and Lies* by Richard Evans, Scribe Publications.

Chapter 5

'Arsenic' in G. D. Parkes (ed.) *Mellor's Modern Inorganic Chemistry*, 1961, pp. 842–843.

'Arsenic poisoning' in J. M. Arena & R. H. Drew (editors) *Poisoning: Toxicology, Symptoms, Treatments,* 5th ed., Charles C. Thomas Publishers, USA, 1986.

Chapter 6

Baselt, R. C. (ed.) (2004) *Disposition of Toxic Drugs and Chemicals in Man,* 7th edition, Biomedical Publications, California, pp. 312–315.

Arkow, P. (1994) 'Animal abuse and domestic violence: Intake statistics tell a sad story', *Latham Letter, 15*(2): 17.

Ascione, Frank R. (1997) 'Battered women's reports of their partners; and their children's cruelty to animals', in: K. Lockwood & S. Ascione (eds) *Cruelty to Animals and Interpersonal Violence: Readings in Research and Application*, Purdue University Press.

McIntosh, S. (2001) 'Calgary research results: Exploring the links between animal abuse and domestic violence', *Latham Letter 22*(4): 14–16.

Ascione, F. R. (2007) 'Emerging research on animal abuse as risk factor for intimate partner violence', in: K. Kendall-Tackett & S. Giacomoni (eds) 'Intimate Partner Violence', Kingston, New Jersey: Civic Research Institute, pp. 3-1–3-17.

Simmons, C. A. & Lehman, P. (2007) 'Exploring the link between pet abuse and controlling behaviours in violent relationships', *Journal of Interpersonal Violence* 22(9): 1211.

Lithgow Mercury, 21 June 2011.

Chapter 7

MIMS 2000 re. 'Serepax' (oxazepam).

Isolation and Identification of Drugs in Pharmaceuticals, Body Fluids and Post-Mortem Material (1974) Volume 1, E. G. C. Clarke (ed.), Pharmaceutical Press, London, p. 458.

(This story appeared in *The Expert Witness: Examinations of Crimes, Drugs and Poisons by a Forensic Toxicologist'*, William J. Allender, New Holland Publishers, Sydney, 2019)

Chapter 8

Pesticide Manual: A World Compendium, 7th edition, (1983), The British Crop Protection Council, Lavenham Press, pp. 5540, 8590.

(This story also appeared as 'Affairs of the Heart and Poisons' in the *Australian Police Journal,* September 2005, vol 59 (3) pp. 141–143)

Chapter 9

Norberg, A., Jones, W. A., Hahn, R. G. & Gabrielsson, J. L. (2003) 'Role of variability in explaining ethanol pharmacokinetics', *Clin. Pharmacokinet.*, 42 (1): 1–31.

Chapter 10

Iwersen-Bergmann, S., Rosner, P., Kuknau, H. C., Junge, M. & Schmoldt, A. (2001) 'Death after excessive propofol abuse', *Int. J. Legal Med.,* 114: 248–251.

Hunter, D. N.; Thornily, A.; Whitburn, R. (1987) 'Arousal from propofol', *Anaethesia* 42: 1128–29.

Follette, J. W. & Farley, W. J. (1992) 'Anesthesiologist addicted to propofol', *Anesthesiology*, 77(4): 817–818.

Fritz, G. A. & Niemczyk, W. E. (2002) 'Propofol dependency in a lay person', *Anesthesiology*, 96(2): 505–506.

Canaday, B. R. (1993) 'Amorous, disinhibited behaviour associated with propofol', *The Journal of Clinical Pharmacology* 12(6): 449–451.

Drummer, O. H. (1992) 'A fatality due to propofol poisoning', *J. Forensic Sci.* 37(4): 1186–1189

Allender, W. J., Anderson, S. G., Perl, J., Jennings, S. 'A Propofol Assisted Death', 48th Meeting of The International Association of Forensic Toxicologists (TIAFT), Bonn, Germany, August 28 – 3 September 2010.

(This story appeared in *The Expert Witness: Examinations of Crimes, Drugs and Poisons by a Forensic Toxicologist*, William J. Allender, New Holland Publishers, Sydney, 2019)

Chapter 11

Milroy, C., Clark, J. C. & Forrest, A. W. (1996) 'Pathology of deaths associated with "ecstasy" and "eve" misuse', *J. Clin. Pathol.*, 49: 149–153.

Conar, D. (2002) 'Ecstasy on the brain', *New Scientist* 20 April 2002, pp 26–33.

(This story appeared in *The Expert Witness: Examinations of Crimes, Drugs and Poisons by a Forensic Toxicologist*, William J. Allender, New Holland Publishers, Sydney, 2019)

Chapter 12

Norberg, A., Jones, W. A., Hahn, R. G., & Gabrielsson, J. L. (2003) 'Role of variability in explaining ethanol pharmacokinetics', *Clin. Pharmacokinet.,* 42 (1): 1–31.

Baselt, R. C. (2004) *Disposition of Toxic Drugs and Chemicals in Man*, 7th Edition, Biomedical Publications, California, pp. 498–501.

Ferra, S. D., Zotti, S., Tedeschi, L. et al (1992) 'Pharmacokinetics of gamma hydroxybutyric acid in alcohol dependent patients after single and repeated doses', *British. J. Clin. Pharm.*, 34:231–235.

Jacobesen, G. (2010) *Abandoned: The Sad Death of Dianne Brimble*, Allen & Unwin, Sydney (This publication provides a more detailed account of this tragedy).

(This story appeared in *The Expert Witness: Examinations of Crimes, Drugs and Poisons by a Forensic Toxicologist*, William J. Allender, New Holland Publishers, Sydney, 2019)

Chapter 13

Norberg, A., Jones, W. A., Hahn, R. G., & Gabrielsson, J. L., (2003) 'Role of variability in explaining ethanol pharmacokinetics: research and forensic applications', *Clin. Pharmacokinet.*, 42(1): 1-31.

Logan, B. K. (2002) 'Methamphetamine – Effects on human performance and behaviour',
  Forensic Sci. Rev. 14: 133–151.

(This story appeared in *The Expert Witness: Examinations of Crimes, Drugs and Poisons by a
Forensic Toxicologist*, William J. Allender, New Holland Publishers, Sydney, 2019)

Chapter 14

Drug Effects on Psychomotor Performance, R. C. Baselt (editor), Biomedical Publications,
  California, 2001, pp. 244–248.

National Institute on Drug Abuse, Methamphetamine DrugFacts, 2019.

Cook, C. E., Jeffcoat, A. R., Sadler, B. M., Hill, J. M. et al (1992) 'Pharmacokinetics of oral
  methamphetamine and effects of repeated daily dosing in humans', *Drug Met. & Disp.*
  20(6): 856–862.

Cook, C. E., Jeffcoat, A. R., Hill, J. M., Pugh, D. E. et al (1993) 'Pharmacokinetics
  of methamphetamine self- administered to human subjects by smoking S-(+)-
  methamphetamine hydrochloride', *Drug Met. & Disp.* 21: 717.

(This story appeared in *The Expert Witness: Examinations of Crimes, Drugs and Poisons by a
Forensic Toxicologist*, William J. Allender, New Holland Publishers, Sydney, 2019)

Chapter 15

Baselt, R. C. (2004) *Disposition of Toxic Drugs and Chemicals in Man*, 7th Edition, Biomedical
  Publications, California, pp. 262–265.

(This story appeared in *The Expert Witness: Examinations of Crimes, Drugs and Poisons by a
Forensic Toxicologist*, William J. Allender, New Holland Publishers, Sydney, 2019)

Chapter 16

Baselt, R. C. (2004) *Disposition of Toxic Drugs and Chemicals in Man*, 7th Edition, Biomedical
  Publications, California, pp. 356–357.

Hallucinogens: A Forensic Drug Handbook (2003), Richard R. Laing (editor), Academic Press.

Pachter, I. J., Zacharias, D. E. & Ribeiro, O. (1959) 'Indole alkaloids of *Acer saccharinum* (the
  silver maple), *Dictyoloma incanescens, Piptadenia colubrina* and *Mimosa hostilis*', *Journal Organic
  Chem.* 24(9): 1285–1287.

A 'furphy' is Australian slang for something that is unlikely, erroneous or improbable.

(This story appeared in *The Expert Witness: Examinations of Crimes, Drugs and Poisons by a
Forensic Toxicologist*, William J. Allender, New Holland Publishers, Sydney, 2019)

Chapter 17

Baselt, R. C. (2004) *Disposition of Toxic Drugs and Chemicals in Man*, 7th Edition, Biomedical
  Publications, California, pp. 66–70.

Matick, H., Anderson, D. & Brumlik, J. (1983) 'Cerebral vasculitis associated with oral
  amphetamine overdose', (1983) *Archives of Neurol*,. 40: 253–254.

Carson, P., Oldroyd, K. & Phadke, K. (1987) 'Myocardial infarction due to amphetamine',
  British Med. J., 294: 1525–1526.

De Silva, D. A., Wong, M. C. & Lee, M. P. et al (2007) 'Amphetamine-associated ischemic
  stroke: clinical presentation and proposed pathogenesis', *J. Stroke Cerebrovasc.*, 16: 185–186.

Lessing, M. P. A., & Hyman, N. M. (1989) 'Intracranial haemorrhage caused by amphetamine
  abuse', *J. Royal Soc. Med.*, 82: 766–767.

El-Mitwall, A. & Malkoff, M. D. (2001) 'Intracerebral hemorrhage', *The Internet J. of Advanced Nursing Pract.*, 4(2): 1–14.

Buxton, N. & McConachie, N. S. (2000) 'Amphetamine abuse and intracranial haemorrhage', *J. Royal Soc. Med.*, 93(9): 472–477.

Goroll, A. H. & Mulley, A. G. (2009) *Primary Care Medicine: Office Evaluation and Management of the Adult Patient*, 6th edition, Lippincott, Williams & Wilkins, chapter 179.

Baselt, R. C. (2004) *Disposition of Toxic Drugs and Chemicals in Man*, 7th Edition, Biomedical Publications, California, pp. 85–88.

Yui, K., Goto, K., Ikemoto, S. et al (1990) 'Increased sensitivity to stress and episode recurrence in spontaneous recurrence of methamphetamine psychosis', *Psychopharmacol.*, 145: 267–272.

Chapter 18

Baselt, R. C. (2004) *Disposition of Toxic Drugs and Chemicals in Man*, 7th Edition, Biomedical Publications, California, pp. 722–725.

Milroy, C., Clark, J. C. & Forrest, A. W. (1996) 'Pathology of deaths associated with "ecstasy" and "eve" misuse', *J. Clin. Pathol.*, 49: 149–153.

Conar, D. (2002) 'Ecstasy on the brain', *New Scientist* 20 April 2002, pp 26–33.

Chapter 19

Baselt, R. C. (2001) *Drug Effects on Psychomotor Performance*, Biomedical Publications, California pp. 244–248.

National Institute on Drug Abuse, Methamphetamine DrugFacts, 2019.

Cook, C. E., Jeffcoat, A. R., Sadler, B. M., Hill, J. M. et al (1992) 'Pharmacokinetics of oral methamphetamine and effects of repeated daily dosing in humans', *Drug Met. & Disp.* 20(6): 856–862.

Cook, C. E., Jeffcoat, A. R., Hill, J. M., Pugh, D. E. et al (1993) 'Pharmacokinetics of methamphetamine self administered to human subjects by smoking S-(+)-methamphetamine hydrochloride', *Drug Met. & Disp.* 21: 717.

Chapter 20

'Janet Fisicaro a "lovely but sad" bride', *The Daily Telegraph,* 21 April 2010.

'Cop who became a killer', *The Sydney Morning Herald*, 19 May 2010.

'British policeman murdered his wealthy Australian wife by throwing her off a cliff', *Daily Mail*, 3 September 2010.

'Wife killer and ex-policeman Des Campbell loses appeal in NSW's highest court', *The Sydney Morning Herald,* 2 September 2014.

'Wife killer Des Campbell loses appeal', *The Australian,* 2 September 2014.

Chapter 21

'Lisa Harnum kept card in pocket to warn friends of Simon Gittany's surveillance, court hears', *The Daily Telegraph*, 17 January 2013.

'"I'll f…ing harm you": Accused murderer allegedly threatened fiancée's counsellor', *The Sydney Morning Herald*, 23 October 2013.

'Balcony death: Police found accused's fingerprint on railing, court told', *The Sydney Morning Herald*, 13 October 2013.

'Video reveals the moments before Lisa Harnum died, and what Simon Gittany did next', *The Sydney Morning Herald*, 1 November 2013.

'Read Justice Lucy McCallum's verdict in full', *The Daily Telegraph*, 27 November 2013.

'Simon Gittany guilty of murdering fiancée Lisa Harnum', *The Sydney Morning Herald*, 27 November 2013.

Dale, A. (2014) *The Fall: How Simon Gittany Killed Lisa Harnum*, Ebury Press, published by Random House, Sydney (This publication provides a very detailed account of this tragedy).

Chapter 22

'Tinder killer met, married and began abusing his partner in New Zealand', *Sunday Star Times*, 22 October 2017.

'Murderer Alexander Villaluna "still angry" about his ex-partner and her Tinder date', *The Sydney Morning Herald*, 22 September 2017.

'Tinder date killer writes apology letter to victim's family', *The Daily Telegraph,* 22 September 2017.

'"I was blinded by my love for her": Man who knifed his ex-wife and murdered Tinder date as they dined refuses to write letter of apology to the dead man's family because he is "still angry about what happened to him"'. Australian Associated Press, 22 September 2017, updated 23 September 2017.

'Husband who stabbed estranged wife's date to death sentenced', *The Daily Telegraph*, 12 October 2017.

'Alexander Villaluna jailed for at least 30 years over Sydney restaurant murder', *The Sydney Morning Herald*, 12 October 2017.

Chapter 23

'Glenn Matthew Cable, 42, jailed after found guilty of attempted murder and jailed for 15 years', *The Courier-Mail*, Australia, 14 April 2014.

'Qld woman basher blames lawyer for verdict', *Brisbane Times,* 1 February 2016.

'Mum almost killed by online date in a vicious baseball bat attack when she broke up with him', *Daily Mail,* Australia, 13 November 2019.

'Mum-of-three reveals how her online date hit her in the head 50 times with a baseball bat when she broke up with him – as she fronts anti-domestic violence campaign', *Daily Mail, Australia*, 31 January 2020.

Chapter 24

'Hannah Baxter dies in hospital after three children killed in suspected murder-suicide in Brisbane's Camp Hill, father Rowan Baxter dies at the scene', ABC Australia, 20 February 2020.

'Camp Hill tragedy: Hannah was "excited" for 2020 with her kids. They only got 50 days', *Brisbane Times*, 20 February 2020.

'Brisbane car fire: Hannah Baxter dies of injuries, three children killed in suspected family violence case', *The Guardian*, 20 February 2020.

'Friend of Hannah Clarke said she was emotionally, financially and sexually abused by estranged husband Rowan Baxter for more than 10 years', *Perth Now*, 21 February 2020.

'Rowan Baxter "couldn't move past the relationship" with Hannah Clarke despite shared custody arrangement, a source reveals', *ABC Australia*, 22 February 2020.

'Killer dad Rowan Baxter who torched wife, 3 kids, was misogynist cheater', *New York Post*, 23 February 2020.

'Mourners hear of Hannah Clarke's lost dreams at Camp Hill vigil', *The Australian*, 23 February 2020.

'Killer Rowan Baxter's creepy stalker tactics: It "was weird"', news.com.au, 27 February 2020.